Practical Handbooks in Archaeology
No 8 (Revised edition)

CHURCHES AND CHAPELS:
investigating places of worship

David Parsons

(University of Leicester)

1998
Council for British Archaeology

1st edition 1989
2nd edition 1998

Copyright © 1998 David Parsons and Council for British Archaeology
All rights reserved

Published 1998 by the Council for British Archaeology, Bowes Morell House, 111 Walmgate, York, YO1 9WA

British Library Cataloguing in Publication Data
A catalogue card for this book is available from the British Library

ISBN 1 872414 97 4

Typeset by Archetype IT Ltd, web site www.archetype-it.com
Printed by Pennine Printing Services Ltd

Front cover: Detail of tracery head from the Flight into Egypt windows, designed by Edward Burne-Jones, *c* 1862, from St Michael and All Angels, Brighton, Sussex
Back cover: Abbey Church, Pershore, Worcestershire from the SW
Photos: David Parsons

Contents

List of Illustrations

Preface to the second edition

A decade has passed since this handbook was first conceived and drafted. In those ten years much has changed, especially in the field of computer technology, and this has affected the way in which professional archaeologists survey and draw historic buildings. Though many of the techniques, and in particular the hardware, are not yet available to the individual investigator or local fieldwork group, it has seemed appropriate to introduce a brief description of them. In many cases the software will become available for use with home computers in the lifetime of this edition. So a new section on Modern Survey and Drawing Methods has been added to Chapter 5.

The bibliography has been updated and expanded. A bit more has been said about redundant churches and Wroxeter (Shropshire) in particular. Otherwise not much has changed. The opportunity has been taken to do some tidying up and make minor corrections which escaped the first time round, including the howler in Fig 13. Local Government Reorganisation has changed our county and district structure yet again, and introduced the concept of the unitary authority. The City of Leicester is no longer in Leicestershire, Rutland is independent again, Brighton and Hove have returned to something like the County Borough status which Brighton enjoyed before 1974. I have tried, with the help of the CBA editorial team, to take account of changes such as these and to make sure that county and other local authority names applied to the places mentioned in this book are correct in post-LGR terms.

David Parsons
Old, Northamptonshire
August 1998

Acknowledgements

Except where the captions indicate otherwise, drawings and photographs are the author's. He is grateful to the following for their permission to take and publish the relevant photographs: Lincoln College, Oxford (Fig 2); the clergy of Cossington (Fig 4), Twywell (Fig 5), Kingsthorpe (Fig 7) and Gaddesby (Fig 21). Mr J P Cryer kindly lent the original of Fig 1, Dr R H White the original of Fig 3, and the late G A Chinnery a usable copy of Herbert's Gaddesby plan (Fig 19). Figs 3, 9, 14, 15 and 18 are Crown Copyright and published with permission of the Royal Commission on the Historical Monuments of England.

The text has benefited from the advice and criticisms of Mr R K Morris (York), Mr C F Stell and Dr G K Brandwood. The Rev W T Snelson and the Rev D L Priston gave help and encouragement in the preparation of Case Studies I and II. My wife, Joan Stephenson, has re-read the first edition with a critical eye, and made valuable suggestions for improvement. Christine Pietrowski of the CBA has (perhaps unwisely) given me *carte blanche* with the second edition, and has been as supportive and helpful as an editor can be. I am grateful to them all.

1 Introduction

This handbook is intended as an aid to the study of places of worship – churches, chapels, meeting houses – whose standing fabric survives in whole or in part. This definition embraces those buildings which were formerly used for worship but which have since been converted to secular use, for example as studios, theatres or commercial premises. For the purposes of this handbook the 'archaeology' of such buildings is taken to mean the evidence of the material remains above ground level, or the 'vertical archaeology' as it is sometimes called. In theory this restriction is at variance with one of the basic tenets of church archaeology, which is that the ideal approach to a standing place of worship should include the below-ground archaeology revealed by excavation, the study of the above-ground fabric by both analytical and art-historical methods, and a full evaluation of the documentary evidence referring to the structure. In practice it is impossible within the scope of a handbook such as this to deal adequately with all three aspects of the archaeological study of churches and chapels. Also, archaeological excavation is both specialist and expensive, and therefore beyond the resources of many readers of this book: its philosophy and techniques have in any case been covered more than adequately by Dr Warwick Rodwell in his excellent *Book of Church Archaeology* (1989). Excavation may be carried out not only as part of a more broadly-based investigation of a standing building, but also in its own right on sites devoid of above-ground structures. In such cases places of worship may be revealed whose existence may be quite unsuspected; these can range from prehistoric ritual structures and Romano-British temples to Christian churches such as those excavated in recent times in Lincoln or at Raunds, Northamptonshire. Sites like these, for which the only evidence comes from excavation, are not discussed in this handbook.

The main emphasis is on the standing structure and how to understand and record it. The fabric can only be understood in relation to the uses to which it is – and has been – put, and those uses are also reflected in the arrangement of the interior and the nature of the permanent or semi-permanent furnishings and fittings. They, too, are discussed in this book. There is also a brief account of the kinds of documentary evidence that should be consulted when investigating a place of worship, though most of what is said here is relevant mainly to churches and chapels of the Church of England. This does not mean, however, that the rest of the handbook is irrelevant to the study of the buildings of Nonconformist, Roman Catholic or other Christian denominations (or, indeed, of non-Christian groups, some of whose places of worship have had a previous use as Christian churches or chapels). The principle of fabric analysis and of the study of furnishings, together with the techniques of recording, apply equally to the buildings of any denomination, sect or group. Because of the author's expertise and experience, many of the examples quoted are Anglican places of worship in the East Midlands, but most readers will find comparable examples fairly readily accessible in Anglican churches and chapels in their own area. There is no lack of Nonconformist buildings of historic interest and worthy of archaeological investigation, but they are often less easily accessible and their officers are less accustomed than Anglican clergy and churchwardens to receiving visits from non-members with archaeological interests.

The range of buildings available for study is enormous. Every denomination has its small rectangular 'boxes' with sparse, simple furnishings. At the other end of the scale are the Anglican and Roman Catholic cathedrals and other major architectural monuments, such as the former abbeys at Selby (N Yorkshire) or Romsey (Hampshire), now serving as Anglican parish churches. These are not considered in this handbook, since their size and complexity and the specialist nature of their documentation puts them beyond the competence of most individuals and local groups. Indeed, many 19th-century urban churches and chapels present quite a challenge to the would-be investigator, with their complexes of vestries, church hall, schoolrooms and meeting rooms, sometimes under the same roof and sometimes detached from the place of worship itself. Between these extremes there is the huge number of village churches and chapels, consisting at the most of a nave and chancel with aisles, a side chapel and perhaps a 19th-century vestry, or of an open worship area with a vestry and a modest residence for a minister or caretaker.

The date-range, and thus the variation in architectural style, is equally great. The Church of England is still using buildings which go back, if not to the time of St Augustine himself, then at least to the end of the 7th century. From the 17th and 18th centuries there are the first chapels and meeting houses purpose-built for Protestant Nonconformist worship. Practically all denominations have a rich heritage of 19th-century buildings, and the provision of new places of worship has continued into the present century, with the emphasis today on multi-purpose buildings, often shared by Anglican and Nonconformist congregations.

With the exception of the most recently built, these churches and chapels have undergone repeated changes over the years. In some cases these have been straightforward enlargements to cope with growing congregations. This is particularly true of Nonconformist chapels which were established at a relatively early date to serve small groups of worshippers, only to be overtaken by the rising popularity of Nonconformity in the late 18th and 19th centuries. Even a superficial browse through the volumes of the *Inventory of Nonconformist Chapels and Meeting Houses* (RCHME/Stell 1986–94) reveals a large number of chapels which had to be extended. The number would be even larger were it not for the frequency with which Nonconformist congregations moved to new premises away from the original site. The medieval church and its Anglican successors had a different attitude to consecrated buildings and sites, so that parish churches have changed their location only rarely, though many were totally rebuilt, particularly in the 19th century. The result is that most Anglican places of worship have remained in continual use for a very much longer period than their Nonconformist counterparts.

The medieval buildings of the Church of England commonly show signs of expansion: one or two side aisles added to a simple rectangular nave, or a chancel lengthened to the east. In addition to these fairly major changes there are usually minor alterations, such as the replacement of windows. The introduction of a whole range of windows above the nave at clerestory level must count as a significant change, however, for it necessitated the removal of the roof and the addition of a considerable number of courses of masonry on top of the existing nave wall; the end result was a complete change in the appearance of the building. Some of these alterations were carried out to provide more space or to make the building more convenient or comfortable to use, but many more were the result of liturgical developments. Side aisles were added to house additional altars and chantry chapels, and chancels were lengthened because of changes in the ritual of the Mass. With the Reformation many of these facilities became redundant, and side chapels, aisles and transepts went out of use almost overnight, unless an alternative use could be found for them. Some continued to be occupied privately by important families, who buried their dead beneath the floor and covered the walls with their memorials. Others, like the south transepts at Castor (Cambridgeshire) or Grimston (Leicestershire), were used as schoolrooms. But those parts of the building for which a new use could not be found were often demolished as soon as maintenance problems developed, if not sooner. The classic examples of such shrinkage are the monastic and collegiate churches of the Middle Ages. When their staffs of monks or clergy were removed in the 16th century the major parts of such churches became redundant and were deliberately sold off for their building materials. In many cases the nave of the church survived the demolition because it served as the parish church, and these rather odd truncated buildings survive today in such places as Fotheringhay (Northamptonshire) or Blyth (Nottinghamshire). More rarely, the east end of the building has survived as the parish church, for example Pershore (Worcestershire) and Boxgrove (W Sussex). At Boxgrove the ruins of the nave still exist to give some idea of the original extent of the building (Fig 1).

Contraction of a comparable kind, though on a smaller scale, can be seen in many Anglican churches and chapels. Side aisles have disappeared and the arcades have been blocked up in the Leicestershire churches of Orton on the Hill and Foston, at Egleton in Rutland and at Ovingdean (Brighton & Hove), where a chapel has also been removed from the south side of the chancel. A whole series of chapels has gone from the south side of the church at Rothwell (Northamptonshire), and at Twywell, in the same county, a chapel or vestry

Fig 1   Boxgrove Priory, West Sussex: view from south-west

has been removed from the north side of the chancel and a transeptal chapel – which had been added to the original building *c*1300 – taken away from the north side of the nave. A list of such removals could be continued *ad infinitum*.

Changes for liturgical reasons have continued in the modern period. The revival in the 19th century of elaborate rituals led to far-reaching fabric restorations, the widespread addition of vestries and the wholesale refurnishing of church interiors. More recently, the modernisation of the liturgy in both Anglican and Roman Catholic churches has produced a spate of internal re-ordering schemes.

At first sight Nonconformist chapels might appear to be less liable to changes of this kind. Most Free Church forms of worship are simpler and more flexible than Anglican or Roman Catholic services, and in many cases they are not enshrined in a formal document like the Prayer Book or Missal. The periodic need for thorough-going reform does not, therefore, arise in quite the same way, though ecclesiastical fashion changes from time to time and may lead, for example, to alterations in the internal furnishings. Financial pressures may also lead to rationalisation. A press report from the late 1980s gives a good indication of what can happen to Nonconformist places of worship:

'Major changes are taking place … The [Baptist church] schoolrooms, which were the original church and date back to 1807, are being sold … the Victorian church building is being updated … in a £140,000 scheme … Alterations … include replacing the pews with chairs and installing a movable partition to divide the church from the ancilliary [*sic*] rooms … lowering the ceiling, and providing new cloakrooms and kitchen. The schoolrooms have planning permission for conversion into flats.' *(Oadby & Wigston Mail,* 29 July 1988, p16)

In addition to this kind of development there are considerable differences of emphasis between the various Free Churches, and a chapel which has changed hands may well have undergone substantial alteration to make it suitable for the practices of its new congregation. For example, a Presbyterian meeting house taken over by Baptists would lose its font in favour of an underfloor baptistery.

All places of worship, of whatever church or denomination, are equally affected by more mundane considerations, in particular the comfort and convenience of the congregation. The addition of porches, the construction of internal lobbies, the installation of electric lighting and central heating, and the screening-off of parts of the worship area to provide meeting rooms, kitchens and lavatories, are or have been common developments in the 20th century. The tendency to subdivide churches and chapels has accelerated as congregations have dwindled. In some places imaginative schemes have been put into effect, whereby part of the building has been converted to living accommodation or office space, leaving a relatively small area available for worship. Increasingly, too, Anglican and Nonconformist places of worship are becoming totally redundant, and new uses have to be found for them. Some, like St Peter Hungate, Norwich, have been converted into museums, others, such as All Saints, Oxford (Fig 2), are now libraries. Other conversions have produced concert halls, theatres, field studies centres, old people's flats, stonemasonry centres, warehouses and even car showrooms. Examples of these and other new uses for redundant churches are given in the SAVE publication *Churches: a question of conversion* (Powell & de la Hey 1987) and a number of older titles. Whatever new use is found for a place of worship, the price of rescuing it from redundancy is usually a great deal of structural alteration as well as the total refitting of the interior. So a further element is added to the archaeological palimpsest which results from the repeated adaptation of a building in use.

Other, perhaps more fortunate, churches simply remain unused. Those of less than average historical interest may be left as 'controlled ruins', and their continued survival depends on whether control or ruination gains the upper hand. Those whose archaeological, architectural or historical significance is greater may be taken on by the Churches Conservation Trust (formerly the Redundant Churches Fund), whose inevitably finite resources are devoted to the maintenance of the buildings and to making them available for public visiting and study. In exceptional cases complete archaeological investigation may accompany the initial stabilisation of the fabric, and both procedures may add considerably to our knowledge of historic places of worship. A classic case is St Peter's, Barton on Humber (N Lincolnshire), where total excavation of the interior was carried out along with a detailed study of the standing fabric. One of the results was the discovery of a hitherto unsuspected Saxo-Norman phase of the church (Rodwell 1989, pp 115–16, ill 49, and *passim*). The evidence in the upstanding fabric that relates to that phase as revealed by

Fig 2   All Saints, Oxford: interior after conversion

excavation could not have been used on its own to demonstrate that such a church existed between the early medieval and late medieval phases represented by the rest of the standing structure. This cautionary tale should be borne in mind while reading Chapter 2 below.

Nevertheless, what exists above ground can tell a significant part of the story, as another redundant church demonstrates. St Andrew's, Wroxeter (Shropshire) became redundant in 1980 and was vested in the then Redundant Churches Fund in 1987. In the meantime, repairs were carried out under the auspices of English Heritage, along with archaeological excavation by Birmingham University Field Archaeology Unit. The excavation was not as extensive as that undertaken at Barton on Humber, but established a number of important developments in the structural history of the church. It did not identify a 'missing' church as the Barton excavations had done, but added a considerable amount of detail to what could be deduced about the structural development by the study of the above-ground archaeology and from historical documents, notably a print of the church made in 1733.

The earliest surviving fabric (Anglo-Saxon) can be identified in the north wall of the nave, whose fabric consists largely of stone blocks salvaged from the dilapidated buildings of the surrounding Roman town of Viroconium. Among the plain ashlars with characteristic lewis and cramp holes are occasional colonette drums, whose ends are easily recognisable because of their circular shape. A straight joint indicates that the church was subsequently extended to the west, probably in the 13th or 14th century (see Fig 3 and the discussion in chapter 2). Between these two phases of the nave, a chancel had been added to the east, rather wider than the nave and surprisingly long for its apparent date. Its surviving windows, including fragmentary examples in the east wall, all but destroyed by the late medieval 'picture' window, indicate a late Romanesque date for this phase. The chancel south doorway has decoration typical of the 12th century, and is partly blocked by a north–south wall, which is all that remains of a later medieval south-east chapel. A west tower was added to the extended nave toward the end of the Middle Ages, but its upper structure seems to date from after the Dissolution of the monasteries, when redundant carved stonework, thought to derive from Haughmond Abbey, was incorporated in all but the lowest stage. The tradition of reusing earlier stonework, whether plain masonry or decorative sculpture, was continued in the post-Reformation period, when part of an Anglo-Saxon cross shaft was incorporated in the upper part of the south nave wall. The date of the wall (1763) and its precise position in the developmental sequence are not apparent from a superficial inspection, but on stylistic grounds it is possible to identify the approximate date of the recycled carved stone. The fabric of the wall is 'an extraordinary mixture of different coloured materials', according to the Churches Conservation Trust's guide book, which leads to the suspicion that a great deal of it may be similarly recycled.

Inside the church there is a great variety of evidence illustrating many points made later in this handbook about the evidence of furnishings and fittings. Among the movable items is a 14th-century wooden chest; the Middle Ages are further represented amongst the fixtures by an Easter Sepulchre in the north wall of the chancel, all but concealed by one of the splendid 16th-century tombs. At the back of the recess forming the sepulchre, which is dated to the 14th century by its ballflower decoration, is a rare, though very damaged, painting of Christ in Majesty, indicating how such furnishings might have appeared in the medieval period. There is a very fine series of tombs of the immediate post-Reformation period, all with much of their original painted finish intact. The furniture of the church illustrates the liturgy of the 17th and 18th centuries, with a Jacobean pulpit, box pews and altar rails dated 1637. The organ, a 19th-century introduction, is mounted on a western galley, originally built in 1772 and later Gothicised. Further fittings visible from inside the church include window glass (a little 15th-century, some 18th, but mostly 19th-century) and six bells ranging in date from 1598 to 1877 and hung in a 17th-century frame in which some 15th-century timbers have been reused.

Wroxeter church forms an ideal introduction to many of the themes which will be dealt with in this handbook. In the chapters which follow it is hoped to demonstrate how to unravel the often complex structural puzzle presented by historic places of worship; to show how the furnishings and fittings contribute to an understanding of the building and the uses to which it has been put; to give an introduction to the documents which can help in the study of a church or chapel; and, finally, to describe the methods which can be used to record the information that results from the study of a place of worship.

Further reading
On the development of the Anglican liturgy: Addleshaw & Etchells 1948 and Yates 1991; on non-liturgical uses: Davies 1968; on Nonconformity: CBA 1985; on new uses for redundant places of worship: Binney & Burman 1977a, 1977b; Dept of the Environment *et al* 1977; on Wroxeter church: White & Barker 1998. General discussions of aspects of church archaeology can be found in Blair & Pyrah 1996 and Parsons 1994.

2 Interpreting the Structure – Observation and Analysis

Unravelling the building history

When the archaeologist first encounters a religious building, it will inevitably have been altered by time, and may bear very little resemblance to its original state. As the Introduction has shown, alterations may have occurred in response to changes in the form of services or their associated activities, or the building may have been adapted to non-religious uses. The archaeologist may set out to inspect a barn or a car showroom and find a converted chapel. The early history of church archaeology is full of such exciting discoveries; the nave of the Anglo-Saxon church at Bradford-on-Avon (Wiltshire) was a school and the chancel a cottage until it was recognised in the mid 19th century for what it was and subsequently restored, while the body of the early church at Bradwell-on-Sea (Essex) was in use as a barn as recently as 1920.

The first essential in the archaeological study of such a building, however slight the change might appear to be, is to establish by means of close examination of the standing fabric what was the original form of the structure and by what stages it reached its present state. This is often referred to by archaeologists as 'structural analysis', though the late H M Taylor (1972) preferred the term 'structural criticism'. It has been objected that 'structural analysis' has a precise technical meaning in the field of engineering, and that the more abstract use of the expression by archaeologists might lead to misunderstanding when communicating with colleagues in related professions. The difficulty is that the periphrases so far proposed are rather clumsy to use and tend to give an inflated idea of the subject, which newcomers to it might find rather daunting. In reality it amounts to nothing more than looking very critically at every available wall surface and feature in the building (including even such unlikely areas as the soffits of arches and the window linings) with the naked eye, unaided by any survey equipment – with the possible exception of a pair of binoculars and a ladder. The object of such a critical inspection is to identify the presence of one or more of a range of diagnostic features which constitute evidence for alterations that have taken place in the building. The individual features may not in themselves be highly significant for the history of the fabric but, in combination, a number of them can form the basis of an extended analysis of the structural history of a building, leading to a provisional interpretation and the preparation of provisional phase plans and elevations, and of hypothetical reconstruction drawings.

The beauty of this kind of analysis is that the recognition of the individual diagnostic features is normally a simple matter and in many cases it is completely objective; yet, while the significance of many of the features is often clear, it can be a mind-bending experience to arrive at an overall analysis which satisfies all the criteria suggested by the evidence. The structural history of a building can be very complex; working it out step by step, however simple the individual stages, can be a very challenging and satisfying exercise.

It is of course true that nothing is ever as straightforward as the textbook suggests. In practice the archaeologist is frequently confronted by immovable furnishings, such as organs or monuments, by locked vestry doors or by layers of plaster and paint, which prevent him from seeing what he most urgently needs to see. Some of these obstacles are insurmountable, as least in the short term (though it is amazing how much can be seen, with practice, 'through' plaster), and the investigator may have to be content with a less-than-complete and, therefore, even more provisional interpretation. It is nevertheless important to establish as far as possible the evidence for fabric changes in the building, using the various diagnostic features which are described here.

Diagnostic features

(a) Straight mortar joints (butt joints)
The so-called 'straight' joint is one of the easiest features to recognise. It depends upon the principle that where walling is built with stones laid in courses (horizontal layers) each stone overlaps the ends of at least two stones in the course below; in its turn it is partially covered by at least two stones in

Fig 3   St Andrew, Wroxeter, Shropshire: photogrammetric record of north elevation
(© Crown Copyright; RCHME)

the course above. This is known as *bonding*, which in brick walling is developed into a variety of different patterns; but whatever the pattern, the principle remains that the individual units in the wall shall interlock to give maximum stability to the structure. A good example of such bonding is shown in the central part of the north elevation of Wroxeter church, which was discussed in Chapter 1 (Fig 3). It is clear from any bonded wall that the vertical or near-vertical joint at either end of any stone does not run up or down the wall beyond the course to which the stone belongs, and this helps the wall to resist any tendency to develop vertical fissures and ultimately to fall apart. It follows that where there are joints which do rise through several courses without interruption, they are unlikely to have been built in that way by the original builders. They are usually the result of extension, rebuilding or repair, in the course of which new walling has been butted up against an already finished edge – a quoin (corner) or the jamb of a window or door, for example. Once again, this phenomenon is well illustrated at Wroxeter, where a straight joint separates the block-work of the eastern section of the nave north wall from the more rubbly masonry to the west (Fig 3). Immediately to the left of the joint is the original north-west quoin of the early nave, to which a western extension was later added. The recognition of such straight or butt joints is often aided by the different appearance of the masonry on either side of it, as at Wroxeter. The stones of the new walling are frequently of different size, shape or colour from those of the old walling (see below, under section d, '*Change of fabric*'). Even where a similar material is used for secondary walling, eg standard bricks, it is frequently the case that the horizontal courses do not match across the line of junction (they do not 'course through'). Such interrupted courses are similar to the more specific *Discontinuous features* discussed below (section c).

Not all continuous mortar lines marking the junction of different phases of walling are either straight or vertical. The best example of a butt joint which is neither, is where masonry has been added above the sloping roof-line of an end wall. The stones immediately below a roof-line are often not cut diagonally to the slope of the roof. When the roof is removed in preparation for the heightening of the wall, the original masonry finishes in an irregular line, which determines the course of the mortar joint between the original and the additional walling. As well as being far from straight, the junction line preserves the diagonal slope of the former roof. In some cases the shape of a complete gable is fossilised below the later walling. A classic example of this is Monkwearmouth church (Sunderland, Tyne & Wear), where the original porch roof-line is still embedded in the west tower; less well known is Cossington (Leicestershire), where the entire gable end of the early nave is clearly visible in the present common nave/tower wall (Fig 4). The church at Bardsey (W Yorkshire), discussed in more detail below, has good examples of both straight vertical and irregular sloping joints.

The discussion of this feature has so far concentrated on coursed masonry. Needless to say, the same kind of butt joint exists in uncoursed (usually

Fig 4   All Saints, Cossington, Leicestershire: interior looking west

rubble) walling, but it is often more difficult to recognise. The identification of the junction between two stretches of random rubble is often very subjective, and the archaeologist seeking to interpret a building with this kind of walling is well advised to seek corroborative evidence from other features in the fabric.

Whatever the exact nature of the evidence, however – whether the walling is coursed or uncoursed, or whether the joint is straight and vertical or not – the implication of the butt joint is always that the areas of masonry on either side of it are of different building phases. Often it is perfectly clear for logical reasons which piece of walling is earlier than the other, but the mortar joint in itself does not provide evidence for the sequence, and other factors may have to be taken into account to arrive at an actual chronology.

(b) Redundant features

Rebuilding implies a change of use, and it is not surprising that some features of the existing building become redundant. Extra rooms built on make original windows superfluous, a new south door makes the old west entrance unnecessary, and even the re-arrangement of furniture can make new openings necessary and old ones surplus to requirements. The heightening of a tower can cover projecting mouldings or carved stones, such as a dedication cross, in the existing masonry, and the removal of a side aisle can leave an arcade with no purpose and the nave potentially exposed to the elements. In many cases it is too troublesome and expensive to remove these redundant features; openings (doors, windows, arches) are usually just blocked up with whatever material comes to hand, and other features are simply left where they are, provided they do not interfere with the new structure or its use.

Blocked openings are usually perfectly easy to recognise. Where the original window, door or arch has shaped stone blocks forming its outline, there is a clear straight joint between the old jamb or head and the blocking material, as described above; but even where the jambs are rubble-built or where the dressed stone 'lining' of the opening has been removed, it is usually possible to detect the junction line, and the difference in the fabric between the general run of the walling and the blocking material is normally quite apparent (see section d below). It is also possible in certain circumstances to spot blocked openings which are covered by plaster or rendering: in the areas of the blocking the plaster may be uneven or (externally) discoloured compared with the surrounding wall surface and it may not adhere properly to dressed stonework, while projecting mouldings not only cause unevenness but may actually protrude through plaster.

An interesting example of redundant openings is provided by the church at Twywell, Northamptonshire (Fig 5). At the east end of the nave north wall there is a blocked arch which formerly led into a transeptal chapel. The outer line of this arch is quite obvious externally, but the evidence inside the church is a little more subtle because the wall is whitewashed over a light skim of plaster. Over the window incorporated into the blocking is a heavy two-order

*Fig 5   St Nicholas, Twywell, Northamptonshire:
exterior of nave north wall with detail of interior*

arch, which is out of proportion with the window embrasure. Despite the wall finish it is possible to trace the continuation of the extrados of this arch to the left of the embrasure and it becomes recognisable as the interior of the entrance to the former transept. Beyond this line, in the 11 o'clock position, it is possible also to see the head of a further blocked opening, this time an early window, of which there is no trace on the exterior of the wall. In form and position it matches the small round-headed window further to the west, and its existence proves that the transept cannot have been an original feature of the church (see section c below). Something of the chronology of the building is already emerging from a brief study of redundant features, and stylistic considerations make it possible to put rough dates on the building phases so far recognised (see section e below). What cannot be dated immediately is the destruction of the north transept and the blocking of its arch. True, the window in the blocking has Y-tracery, which suggests a date around 1300, but this is too close to the 13th/14th century date of the double-chamfered transept arch to allow a credible life-span for the building before its demolition. The most likely explanation is that the window originally belonged to the fabric of the transept itself and is, therefore, of the same date as the blocked arch; at the time of the demolition the window was salvaged and incorporated in the blocking. Another possible explanation is that the window was inserted in the 19th century, but this would need to be substantiated from documentary sources (see Chapter 4). In neither case does the window provide evidence for the date of demolition which, in common with the removal of other major components of medieval churches, such as aisles, is most likely to have taken place after the Reformation, perhaps as late as the 18th century. In the 16th century the multiplicity of altars, which had been common in churches during the Middle Ages, was reduced drastically to a single communion table, and the parts of the building designed to house them became instantly redundant. Chapels, transepts and aisles which were not rescued by becoming family chapels or mausolea would be considered for demolition as soon as their maintenance became a financial embarrassment to the parish.

Another major structural element of the parish church which is subject to change is the roof. Changing fashions and carpentry techniques and the use of different covering materials (lead, thatch, tiles, shingles) may lead to the redesigning of the timber framework of the roof, often involving an alteration in the pitch (the angle of slope). In the late medieval period a frequent cause of reroofing was the addition of a clerestory stage to the walls of the nave; in the process, the existing roof would have to be dismantled entirely and a new one constructed at the height of the new wall-top, though this might consist of the old timbers reassembled. Evidence for the former existence of such abandoned roofs and, of course, for their pitch (which may imply the use of a certain kind of covering) is often preserved in the fabric of the building, simply because it was not worth anyone's while to remove it. It consists of the weatherproof seal between the end of the roof and the part of the building which it abutted;

typically this occurs at the junction of a nave roof and a tower, but similar evidence may be found where roofs of porches, vestries, transepts, chancels, etc, once joined the body of the church. The purpose of the seal was to prevent rainwater running down the face of the wall from seeping through the crack between the end of the roof and the wall itself, and thus penetrating into the interior of the building (Fig 6). It normally took one of two forms, either a projecting strip of stonework built into the wall, known as a 'weathering', or a groove cut into the wall, into which a strip of lead flashing was originally mortared.

The implications of this form of evidence are somewhat different from those of the superficially similar trapped gable (see above, p 19 and Fig 4). Apart from the obvious information about the vanished roof or succession of roofs, redundant weatherings or flashing grooves may tell us significant things about the other parts of the building. For example, they often indicate not only that the present clerestorey is a secondary feature, but also that the building, despite having side aisles, originally had no clerestorey at all. At Ketton (Rutland) it is possible to relate the height and pitch of one of the weatherings to those of trapped half-gables at the west end of the side aisles and thus to conclude that in the 13th century the whole church was covered by one vast roof, stretching from the nave ridge to the aisle walls, and with little or no change of pitch as it passed over the nave arcades. This would have given the church a totally different appearance from anything we are currently familiar with, and this realisation is important for the three-dimensional reconstruction of churches, especially in the early medieval period (see below, p 41 and Fig 14). Another fairly common observation is that an old roof line on a tower is not symmetrical to the nave, which may mean that one of the side walls has been moved; the implications for the whole structural history of the church can be far reaching.

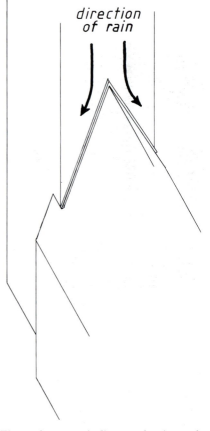

direction of rain

Fig 6   *Axonometric diagram showing roof weathering on face of tower*

Fig 7   St John Baptist, Kingsthorpe, Northampton:
interior of nave and chancel from south-west

(c) Discontinuous features

While some features are merely made redundant by rebuilding, others are destroyed in whole or in part. Partially destroyed or 'interrupted' features are useful pointers to building history. The classic example of this kind of evidence is the window or series of windows in an original outside wall cut by an arch or arcade leading into an adjacent part of the building (eg side aisle) added on later (Fig 7). Not only do such intersections prove that the adjacent chamber *is* secondary, but they also furnish the basic chronologies on which general style sequences (typologies) are built.

Similar information may be given by discontinuities in linear features: plinths, string courses, decorative friezes, etc, running horizontally, and buttresses or pilasters running vertically. The principle here is similar to Newton's first Law of Motion, which states that a body will continue in uniform motion in a straight line unless acted upon by an external force: a linear architectural feature will continue in a logical fashion to the limits of the fabric to which it belongs unless interrupted by a reconstruction or an addition to the building. Vertical features usually run from the base of the wall to the eaves, or are contained by contemporary horizontal features. Plinths, string courses and friezes normally run round a complete building in a continuous line, and if they break off illogically or if their profile changes markedly it is usually a sign of rebuilding or of an addition to the fabric. For example, the projecting

Fig 8   St Michael, Diseworth, Leicestershire: nave north wall,
detail of plinth, showing abrupt change of profile

vertical strips in the nave wall at Dymock (Gloucestershire) break off at
different levels below the wall-top and the irregular line which joins their ends
marks off an area of plane walling that has clearly been rebuilt; at Diseworth
(Leicestershire) the change in the plinths from a low stepped profile to a tall,
more complex section marks the point at which the nave was considerably
lengthened in the Middle Ages (Fig 8).

(d) Changes of fabric
The kinds of evidence so far described are frequently complemented by
changes in the nature of walling; such changes can also occur independently of
the other diagnostic factors and stand by themselves as evidence for the
development of the building. They are sometimes gross contrasts, such as that
illustrated by Figure 3, but more often they depend on differences in colour,
small variations in texture or in the surface finish produced by different cutting
tools, or simply the way the stones are laid in the matrix of the wall. They are
thus difficult to describe in words and almost impossible to illustrate adequately. The best way to learn to recognise fabric changes is to study a large
number of buildings at first hand, preferably in the company of someone who
is already used to observing this kind of evidence. The subtlety of fabric
changes is well illustrated by such churches as Bishopstone (E Sussex), where
almost all the plain walling consists of flint nodules in a mortar matrix; it is

Fig 9   St Andrew, Bishopstone, East Sussex: view from south-west
(© Crown Copyright; RCHME)

nevertheless possible to define several fabrics of different periods, ranging from totally random (uncoursed) rubble to the very neatly coursed masonry of the west tower and the regimental regularity of the 19th-century rebuild of the south aisle (Fig 9).

Despite the difficulty of explaining fabric characteristics, the following check-list may form a useful starting point for recognising different types of walling:

type of stone – general geological identification, eg, limestone, granite, flint, mixed assemblage;

colour of stone – often a function of geological type; 'secondary' colouring developed by weathering, lichens, etc, relevant, since different stones discolour differently in identical conditions;

size and shape – are the stones cut to shape? with sharp or rounded corners? whole pebbles or quarry waste? etc;

tooling – surfaces of stones may show marks of finishing tool – saw, chisel, bolster, etc: are they all similar?

method of laying – coursed or random; counterpitched (herringbone) or other special techniques; narrow or wide mortar joints.

Unfortunately it is easy to overinterpret fabric changes. They do not necessarily indicate a new building period but could result from the use of a new load of stone, especially where demolition material is being reused. The somewhat piebald appearance of many medieval walls often requires no further explanation than that the masonry was usually covered with plaster inside and rendering outside. The west tower at Kingsthorpe (Northamptonshire) changes dramatically halfway up from the ironstone to limestone, but in the Middle Ages this change was probably disguised by rendering over the lower stages, giving a general 'white' appearance to the whole tower. Whether or not the upper part was rebuilt has to depend on other criteria.

(e) Inconsistencies
Churches are built by people, and people cannot be relied on always to act in a rational manner. Certain features in a building may be the result of personal whim; a tower may be heightened or new furniture installed with the sole purpose of keeping up with the Joneses of the next parish. Nevertheless the various parts of a church have specific functions to perform, and these tend to determine the layout, design and detailed execution at the time of the initial building.

The plan and individual features of an original church or its constituent parts may be expected to be consistent with the purpose for which the building was intended. Obvious inconsistencies often point to the adaptation or extension of a building in order to fit it to changing needs or circumstances. Three general areas of inconsistency, illogicality or incongruity can be identified: peculiarities of layout or design, functional illogicality and stylistic incongruity.

Design peculiarities: oddities in the plan of a church are always worth noting. An apparent peculiarity of layout can be produced by the addition of side aisles to a simple church consisting originally of a nave with a narrower chancel. It is quite common to find the aisles continuing past the east end of the nave to overlap the chancel. This gives the effect of a 'dog leg' in the side walls of the main body of the church which would almost certainly have been avoided if the building had been designed with through-aisles from the start. Examples of this feature are the churches at Kingsthorpe in Northampton and Burley-on-the-Hill (Rutland; Fig 10). The salient east angles of the nave are clearly shown on the plan and are equally clear when seen in elevation from the eastern ends of the aisles of the churches concerned. In many cases it is possible to recognise the quoin stones of what was originally an exterior angle of similar building. The inescapable conclusion is that the aisles of the church are secondary features and that the building originally consisted simply of the nave and narrower chancel. In the case of Kingsthorpe this interpretation is

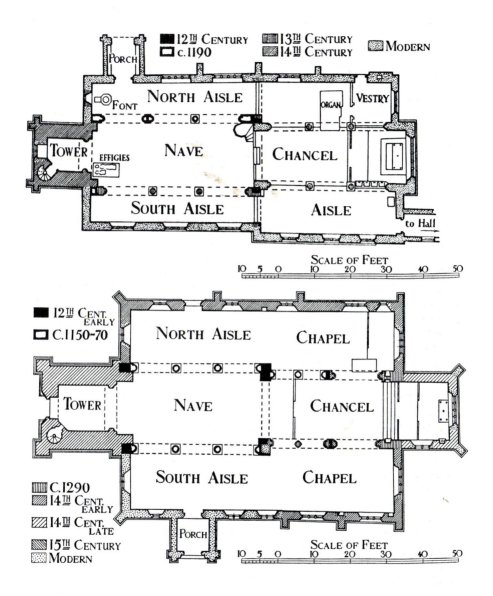

Fig 10 Plans of St John Baptist, Kingsthorpe, Northampton, and Holy Cross,
Burley, Rutland (after VCH Northamptonshire, 4, 85, and VCH Rutland, 2, 118; courtesy
University of London Institute of Historical Research)

confirmed by the evidence of the arcades in both nave and chancel cutting earlier windows (see Fig 7). At Burley there is also evidence in the arcades, but of a more subtle kind. Between the central and western arches of the north arcade there is not a circular column supporting the wall above, as there is one bay further east, but a pier consisting of a short stretch of plain walling with a half-round respond on both its east and west faces. Such seemingly illogical pieces of walling interrupting an arcade are sometimes interpreted as the remains of cross walls dividing off the aisles, but this often leads to difficulties in understanding the building as a whole. A more universally applicable interpretation seems to be that inserted arcades often did not fit the walls into which they were built. The dimensions of an arch, especially the semicircular type mainly used up to c 1200, are not easily adjustable, since they depend on the size of the available wooden centring and the shape of existing templates for cutting the individual voussoir stones of the arch head. Small wonder, then, that groups of arches often could not be made to fit exactly a wall not originally designed to take them; the simple solution to the misfit was to leave a short piece of plain wall, often at one or other end of the arcade, but occasionally between adjacent arches, as at Burley.

Functional illogicality: here the principle is that most architectural features have a practical purpose, and if they are observed in positions where they cannot perform their function, some alteration to the building may be assumed. For example, windows are normally intended to transmit light from the exterior to the interior of a building; it is not logical for them to connect two interior spaces, and when they are found in an internal wall this is a clear indication that one of the units of the building has been tacked on to the other. Since windows in this sort of position are in many cases cut by inserted arches (see above, p 25), the argument from logic is unnecessary, but there are many examples in which the original outer wall has been left intact and the uselessness of the window is the main indication of the earlier form of the building. Other typically external features, when found inside, tell the same story. Exterior mouldings are deliberately shaped to throw off water running down the face of a wall, and thus have no logical place on an internal wall. Genuine interior mouldings are decorative rather than functional. In addition to these mechanical aspects of the building, there are other features – often internal features – whose function has to do with the uses to which the church was put. As the next chapter will explain (see below p 50) the presence of a now redundant piscina indicates the position of a former altar at some time in the Middle Ages. At Twywell (Northamptonshire) such a piscina is preserved, apparently illogically, in the outside north wall of the chancel. What is unusual here is the implication of an altar in the open air. Since the Christian altar needs to be sheltered beneath a roof, the interpretation of the Twywell feature must be that on the north side of the chancel there was formerly a chapel or sacristy, for which there is otherwise no direct archaeological evidence.

Stylistic incongruity: the succession of architectural styles (at least from the Norman conquest to the 19th century) and the characteristics of each style are so well known that it is easy to see when features of different types are mixed in one apparently homogeneous wall, unit or building. Examples of this range from the obvious juxtaposition of Romanesque and Early English blind arcading on the west front of Lincoln cathedral to the often glaring intrusion of Victorian features into so many medieval parish churches restored in the 19th century, eg the chancel arch at Kingsthorpe surrounded by masonry of largely 'Norman' style (Fig 7). The recognition of the rebuilding implied by this stylistic incongruity reveals, in fact, more than the 'standard' Victorian restoration; the actual position of the chancel arch was altered, and the use and furnishing of the various parts of the church adjusted accordingly.

Further reading
On building techniques and materials: Clifton-Taylor 1987, Salzman 1967; on ecclesiastical architectural history: Cox 1914, Bond 1905; for the analytical approach to church buildings any of the publications of Robert Willis in the 19th century or of A Hamilton Thompson in the 20th.

Case Study I

No one building can be expected to show all the diagnostic features described in this chapter, but the church chosen for this brief case study illustrates several of them. What follows is an example of how the various features can be used in combination to arrive at a provisional interpretation of the building as a whole. It is also a demonstration of how much information can be obtained from the study of a single elevation, but it must be emphasised that the interpretation is only a partial one, which is likely to be modified by information obtained from other parts of the fabric, from excavation or from documentary sources.

All Hallows, Bardsey, West Yorkshire
This church in the north-east environs of Leeds is a classic case of development from relatively simple beginnings to a more complex medium-sized village church. The present building consists of a nave of three bays with a west tower and a typically long late medieval chancel. Side aisles, spacious for a church of this size, flank the nave, overlapping the tower. Beyond the north aisle is a chapel about half the length of the chancel and to the east of the south aisle there is a slightly shorter chamber which currently houses the organ.

Perhaps the most striking features of the west elevation (Fig 11) are the straight joints between the tower and the side aisles. The lack of bonding is emphasised, particularly at the height of the main range of windows, by the

Fig 11 *All Hallows, Bardsey, West Yorkshire: exterior west elevation*

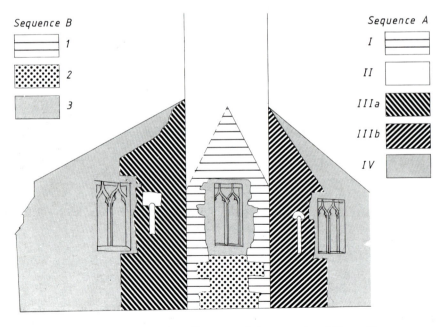

Fig 12 *All Hallows, Bardsey: diagrammatic interpretation of Figure 11*

contrast between the small neat stones of the aisle masonry and the much larger blocks of stone in the tower fabric. Above the level of the window heads this contrast is much less marked, but the difference in the fabrics – the walling of the aisles is somewhat wider jointed – is apparent even in monochrome reproduction. In reality, variations of colour tend to emphasise the slight changes in the stonework. It is clear, on account both of fabric differences and of the butt joints, that the tower and the side aisles were built at different times. Logic demands that the tower should be earlier in date, since it is impossible to imagine a building where the ends of the aisles project beyond the nave, leaving a space between them. An earlier phase in the development of the church can therefore be immediately recognised, in which the building was an aisleless structure with a west tower standing free on three sides. This stage is represented in the development diagrams (Fig 13) by the Phase I plan. As will become clear, this plan also applies to Phase II.

Returning to the picture of the west elevation, it is noticeable that the fabric of the tower itself is not homogeneous. This can be seen most clearly by following the masonry adjacent to the straight mortar joint – that is, the original quoins of the tower. At ground level there are the large sharply-cut blocks mentioned already, but at the height of the head of the two-light window much smaller stones take over, and run up the quoins beyond the point where the aisle roof abuts on either side to the top of the picture (and ultimately to the top of the tower, not shown in the illustration). Such an abrupt change in the character of the quoining almost invariably indicates two phases of building, but only the slightest change in the ordinary walling of the tower can be distinguished at the appropriate level. What can just be made out, however, is a faint diagonal line beginning at the lightning conductor, about two courses above the window, and running just to the right of a very small white stone midway between the two-light window and the rectangular one in the upper part of the tower. This feature is not very clear in Figure 11, though the original photograph, taken in 1971, does just show it. Admittedly it is difficult to see it today on site, but it was much clearer on my first visit to Bardsey in about 1960, as a transparency taken on that occasion still shows. Dr Taylor, in his Bardsey entry in *Anglo-Saxon Architecture* (1965), comments that it was easier to see on the occasion of his original visit in 1937 than when he revisited in 1958. The diagonal line may therefore be accepted as evidence on good authority, though if one were relying solely on current observation there would be some doubt about its existence. This indicates both that there is a high degree of subjectivity in the visual analysis of a structure, and that the diagnostic features on which it is based are not permanent or permanently visible. This is a point which will be taken up in Chapter 5.

The interpretation of the diagonal line is, paradoxically, clearer than the feature itself. Taken in conjunction with the change of quoining technique it indicates that the earlier, lower, part of the tower was surmounted by a gable,

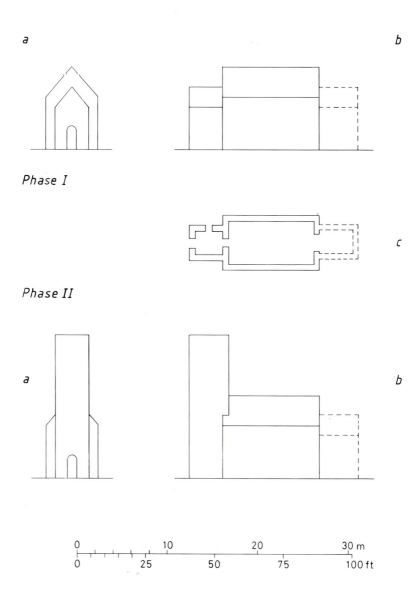

a

b

Phase I

Phase II

c

a

b

0   10   20   30 m

0   25   50   75   100 ft

Fig 13   All Hallows, Bardsey: development plans and elevations

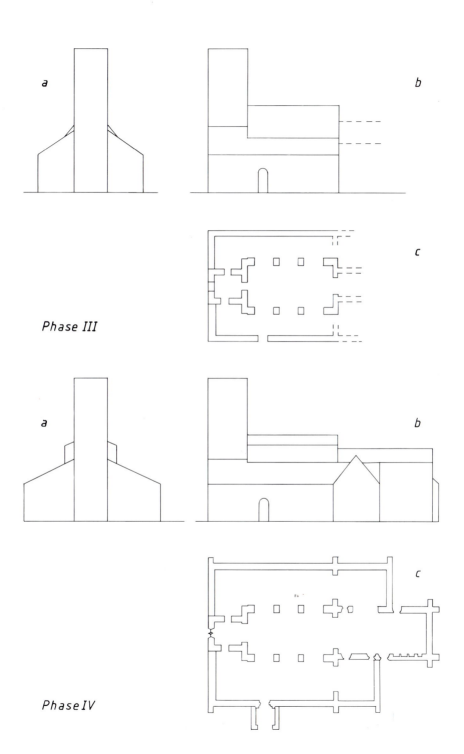

a

b

c

Phase III

a

b

c

PhaseIV

which implies a saddleback roof at this level. In short, the original structure at the west end of the church was a porch. Above and behind this porch the upper walling and west gable of the nave would have been visible, as shown in elevation diagram Ia of Figure 13. In due course, the roof of the porch was removed and, without destroying the gable, further masonry with small quoin stones was added to continue the porch wall upward in the form of a tower (Fig 13, elevation IIa). Since the straight mortar joints are continuous from ground level to the aisle roofs, the aisles are later than the upper part of the tower, just as they are later than the lower part, or porch. They therefore form a third phase in the overall sequence.

The aisles in their turn were subsequently altered. The evidence is clearer on the south side, where from the point at which the aisle roof abuts the tower, a steep double diagonal line runs towards the top left corner of the two-light window. Apart from a colour change in the fabric, there is no complementary evidence in the south aisle walling. On the north side the line of what must have been an earlier roof pitch is much more ragged, but appears to end two or three courses above the centre of the two-light window. Below the window, and partly hidden by the shrub (no longer there in 1987!), there is a suspicion of a vertical straight joint, which fortunately can be confirmed by reference to the east elevation of the north-east chapel, where there is a clear vertical joint in the corresponding position, with a matching plinth change. It is therefore apparent that the north aisle – and by implication the south – had been considerably widened. This has made necessary the adjustment to the roof pitch indicated by the evidence above the windows.

It is now possible to summarise the main phases of the development of Bardsey church, as indicated by the features of the west elevation. The interpretation diagram (Fig 12) represents this schematically. In its first phase the church had a west porch projecting from the west elevation of the nave. In phase II the porch was raised to form a west tower, but the church remained otherwise unchanged. In the third phase the relatively narrow side aisles were added, overlapping the west tower and butting up against its quoins. On the evidence of the west front it is not possible to be sure whether or not the aisles were added simultaneously. However, it may be noted that the heads of the narrow windows that belong to this phase are not identical: in the north aisle the large block of stone forming the head is shaped only to form the intrados, or inner curve, of the arch, while the south aisle window (which, incidentally, is slightly taller) has a smaller stone head carved to form both intrados and extrados. Those differences are suggestive rather than diagnostic, but the possibility of different construction dates for the two aisles must be borne in mind. This possibility is allowed for in the diagram by the subdivision, with appropriate hatching, into phases IIIa and IIIb. Finally in phase IV, the two aisles were extended outwards. This phase has not been subdivided though there is no fabric evidence for the simultaneous extension of both aisles. However, if the two-light windows belong to the masonry of this phase, rather than being later insertions, their close similarity in all respects implies one building campaign in which both aisles were enlarged together.

These four phases, with their subdivisions, are the main steps in the overall development of the church structure ('Sequence A' in Fig 12). Within the west elevation, however, there is a minor development, referred to in the interpretation diagram as 'Sequence B'. This sequence is contained entirely within the fabric of the porch (A, phase I) and is not directly related to any other fabric or phase of the main sequence. If the main porch fabric is regarded as phase 1 in sequence B, phase 2 is represented by the masonry between the quoin stones up to a height of about 1.5m. This masonry does not seem to relate organically to the quoins, indeed it stands a little proud of the strictly defined plane between the quoin stones. Again, this is a somewhat subjective observation, but it is strengthened by the knowledge that a porch must have had an external entrance in its original form. As the phase plans show, north and south entrances to the tower still exist within the present church, and one of them may have been an external doorway originally. If so, there was no physical necessity to have a west entrance, but the other early porch with side doors (Monkwearmouth) also has a west doorway, and it is possible that Bardsey was similarly provided. If this analogy is correct, then the fabric of the west entrance must have been removed before the opening was blocked with masonry B2. Phase 3 of this sequence, by contrast, is unmistakable. The intrusive masonry around the two-light window points quite clearly to the insertion of this feature.

The tentative establishment of these two sequences is as much as one can derive from the study of the west elevation alone. In fact, it has already been necessary to refer to other parts of the building and to buildings elsewhere in order to help the argument. The sequences cannot be any further refined and absolute dates for the various phases cannot be proposed without reference to other evidence, in particular to accepted stylistic characteristics.

The easiest part of the fabric to pinpoint stylistically is the upper part of the tower (phase AII). The belfry opening of two lights in the south wall is of typically late Anglo-Saxon form that seems not to survive the Norman Conquest to any significant extent. The conventional date for this phase is therefore 10th–11th century. Nothing specific can be said about phase I, except that it must be of some earlier date in the Anglo-Saxon period. The analogy of Monkwearmouth quoted above suggests a possible 7th- to 8th-century date, though this is little more than guesswork. Phase III, the north and south aisles in their original form, is characterised by the narrow round-headed windows of the west elevation. Their simple form is characteristic of 'Romanesque vernacular', and would not be out of place in either an Anglo-Saxon or a Norman context. This phase of the building must be later than the late Anglo-Saxon belfry openings. Assuming that the arcades in the nave side walls do not replace earlier ones, they indicate that the aisles were added in the 12th century. Stylistically, the north and south arcades are not identical. The south arcade shows elements of the transition to the Gothic style and is therefore of later date that the north arcade. This indicates the order in which the aisles were added. The north aisle (phase IIIa) came first, and may be assigned to the 12th century (a more specific date would depend upon a comparative analysis of the features of the north arcade). The south aisle (phase IIIb) was added later in the same century. As for the extension of the aisles in phase IV, it has already been noted that the two-light windows of the west elevation imply that both aisles were dealt with at the same time. In fact, similar windows are to be seen in the other elevations of the church and this suggests a major unifying building campaign at whatever date the style of the windows indicates. Unfortunately they are of a fairly standard pattern, which could occur at any time from the development of the ogee arch in the 14th century to the end of the Middle Ages, a period of at least 200 years. The most that can be said for phase IV is that it is 'late medieval'.

The late medieval rebuild also affected the early medieval porch/tower, into which one of the two-light windows was inserted (phase B3). The surrounding phase 1 belongs – equally vaguely – to the early Anglo-Saxon period. The postulated infilling of the putative west door (phase 2) presumably belongs to a time when alternative access to the church was arranged. In practice this means a south door in the body of the church, or possibly opposed north and south doorways. In the late medieval south wall of the south aisle such a doorway still exists, though it is not in its original place. Its stylistic details are consistent with its belonging to the fabric of the late 12th-century south aisle, and it must have been preserved when the aisle was widened, and incorporated in the new south wall. The church, then, had a south entrance by the end of the 12th century at the latest, so that the equation of phase B2 with AIIIb would not be unreasonable. The abandonment of the west entrance could have been earlier than this, however, and might have been part of a reorganisation associated with the conversion of the porch into a tower (phase II).

The information drawn from the fabric is summarised below in tabular form. It must be emphasised that this interpretation is a provisional one which would require revision in the light of other evidence that may become available. In particular, excavation within the church might be expected to extend greatly the number of phases and sub-phases, as investigations at Wharram Percy and other churches have shown. Much more complexity might be expected of a building which has existed for more than 1000 years. Certain features discussed in this case study are capable of other interpretations, eg the 'porch' gable line, which may be a slippage line due to subsidence, and it is possible to make out a case for structural phases not considered here, such as the possibility that the Anglo-Saxon porch/tower was originally flanked by *porticus*. Such alternative interpretations are not ruled out by the present case study, which is offered as a specimen exercise in interpretation on the understanding that it is not to be regarded as definitive, but as a personal contribution to the ultimate unravelling of Bardsey's building history.

Provisional Chronology of All Hallows' Church, Bardsey

Sequence A	Sequence B	Provisional Date
Phase I	Phase 1	Early Anglo-Saxon
Phase II	↑	Late Anglo-Saxon
Phase IIIa	?Phase 2	12th century
Phase IIIb	↓	Late 12th century
Phase IV	Phase 3	14th-early 16th century

Note: I am grateful to Mr Peter Ryder (formerly West Yorkshire Archaeological Service) for sharing his observations at Bardsey church with me and for discussing their interpretation with me in great detail.

Chapter 3: Furnishings and Fittings

When studying a church or chapel it is not sufficient to understand the basic structure (usually masonry or brick, but in certain areas like Cheshire the walls are sometimes timber-built). The furnishings and fittings play a central role in making the building usable for its specialist purposes. What follows can be only a brief introduction to a subject that has its own copious literature, to which the reader is referred for more detailed information.

Elements of the structure
(a) Roofs
Some aspects of the roof – evidence for its height and pitch, and for its relation to the development of the building – have been touched on above (pp 23–4). Roofs also have their own developmental sequence which can be studied in its own right. Traditional typological assessments are now being supplemented by the more specific study of carpentry techniques (Cecil Hewett and others) and by the application of dendrochronology. What follows cannot pretend to be even a summary of this rather specialist field; it is no more than an introductory outline, and a subjective one at that.

Early medieval church roofs rarely survive except as a collection of individual timbers reused in later structures. The evidence of old weathering strips, already discussed, shows that they were usually of fairly steep pitch and that in aisled churches they rose from the nave wall-top, often without the interposition of a clerestory. Side aisles were usually quite narrow, and presumably always had lean-to roofs. There is some evidence to suggest that in many cases the nave and side aisles were covered by a single roof, which swept down in a continuous line from the ridge above the centre-line of the nave to the top of the (often very low) aisle wall. The church at Polebrook in Northamptonshire is thought to have had a roof of this kind in the 13th century (Fig 14, compare Ketton, p 24 above; there is comparable evidence at Castor, in the Soke of Peterborough (Cambridgeshire)), and examples still survive in several places, such as Alfold (Surrey) (Fig 15). The so-called 'cat-slide' roof was not an appropriate form in the late Middle Ages, however, when it became fashionable to add a clerestory range to the nave walling. This made it necessary to have separate roofs for the nave and the side aisles. From the mid-13th century on, side aisles also tended to become more spacious and in place of a pent or lean-to roof they sometimes had saddle-back roofs of variable pitch.

The frequent occurrence in early naves (up to the 13th century) of a doorway high in the end wall, with its threshold at exactly the right level to coincide with the tie beam of the original roof, implies both that this closed kind of roof structure was common at this period (Fig 16) and that the beams might have been boarded over, giving a usable attic to which the high door would have given access. If this is correct, the nave of an early medieval church would have had a flat ceiling (perhaps even with further boarding under the beams), which would have given a totally different appearance and different acoustic qualities from those which are familiar today.

Later in the Middle Ages more open roof structures seem to have become more common – at all events the high doorways finally disappeared in the 14th century. In some parts of the country, notably East Anglia, many of the more imposing churches acquired elaborate roofs of hammerbeam design (Fig 17). Toward the end of the medieval period more modest churches in particular had nave roofs of a very low pitch, with the purlins and rafters resting more or less directly on a cambered tie beam, but in many cases the whole roof was now at a higher level because of the addition of a clerestory. After the Reformation roofs continued generally to be of low pitch, but the 17th and 18th

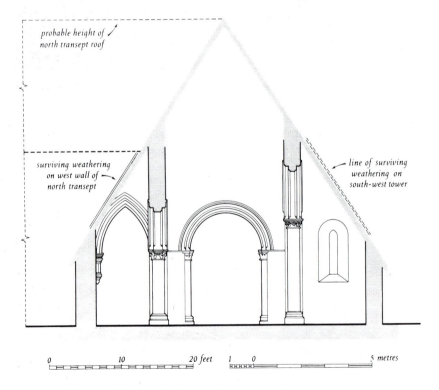

Fig 14 All Saints, Polebrook, Northamptonshire: reconstructed section (© Crown Copyright; RCHME, Northamptonshire Inventory, 6, fig 172)

Fig 15 St Nicholas, Alfold, Surrey: view from north-west (© Crown Copyright; RCHME)

centuries saw the reintroduction of the ceiling inside the church, usually made of plaster and sometimes very elaborate in its design. Many of the church roofs that we see today, however, are the product of the 19th-century restorers, who tended to revert to the 'original' roof pitch and to do away with internal ceilings.

It is therefore not very profitable to discuss in any detail the materials with which roofs were originally covered. Something can be deduced from the pitch of the roof, and Clifton-Taylor (1987) makes some very useful observations about angles appropriate to various covering materials. The choice of a roof pitch in relation to any given material is dictated both by the ability of the material to shed water effectively and by the most appropriate method of attaching the covering to the roof structure. For example, it is clear that thatch needs a steep pitch to be able to drain properly, otherwise the straw or reeds will end up as a soggy mass of decaying (and very heavy) material; but this has implications for the method of attaching the covering to the roof, since it cannot simply be hung on pegs like tiles or slates. These last two materials are more versatile, and can be hung on roofs of varying pitch. However, Clifton-Taylor and other writers tend to overemphasise the extent to which lead requires a roof of low pitch. For the early medieval period there is consistent structural evidence for steeply pitched roofs and at the same time considerable documentary evidence for the use of lead. Some sources make it clear that the lead was applied as shingles, ie small flat plates, which are not subject to 'creep', as sheet lead is, when used on a steep roof. This received

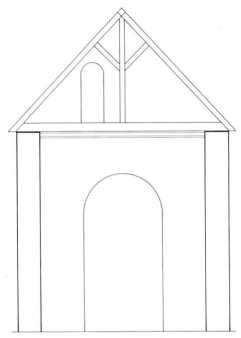

Fig 16 St Mary Magdalen, Tixover, Rutland: reconstructed roof section and view of nave interior west elevation (courtesy Royal Archaeological Institute)

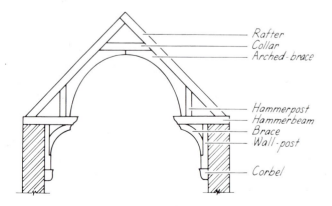

Fig 17 Diagrammatic section of simple hammerbeam roof (after Cocke et al 1996, fig 40e)

tangible confirmation in the shape of a few such 'tiles' of lead excavated in 1987 north of the cathedral at Rouen. These were discovered in a 9th-century demolition layer, but ascribed to the roof of a building dating to the 6th or 7th century. They have the dimensions and appearance of ceramic roofing *tegulae* of the Roman period, with the flange on one side continued as a half roll to fulfil the function of the separate *imbrex* of Roman roofing. Since lead is such an eminently recyclable material, this evidence is extremely rare, and it was a stroke of good luck to discover it. Valuable in its own right, it also serves as a warning that extrapolation from modern practice can be misleading.

(b) Wall finishes

After the plaster-stripping activities of the Victorian restorers it is hard to imagine how common it was for medieval (and post-medieval) walls to be rendered both inside and out. Even major churches built of good ashlar masonry were given a thin skim of plaster internally, on which were then laboriously painted thin dark red lines representing the 'joints' between false 'ashlars'; in the middle of each was also painted a stencilled rosette or similar pattern. This early medieval form of decoration is preserved, for example, in Durham Cathedral, and more or less fragmentary versions of it appear in very many parish churches. For example, the soffit of one of the south arcade arches at Wartnaby (Leicestershire) is decorated in this way, while the rest of the arcade has painted scrolls and triangles. At Burton Latimer (Northampton-shire) part of the north aisle wall is lined out as a background to figural scenes, but there are no rosettes painted on the false 'stones'.

Remains of more ambitious schemes of decoration survive surprisingly often, though much has inevitably been destroyed. Life cycles of Christ and portraits of the saints were popular subjects for wall paintings in the Middle Ages and were prime targets for the iconoclasts of the post-Reformation period. From the Restoration of Charles II, however, attitudes were less hard and pictorial mural painting reappears in the form of delightful cartouches with Old Testament prophets or the Ten Tribes of Israel, as at Astbury (Cheshire) or Burton Latimer (Northamptonshire). Panels with the Royal Arms were *de rigueur* and are sometimes painted direct on to the plaster. At almost every period texts could be painted, culminating in the uplifting banner mottoes of the 19th century. The High Victorian period also produced elaborate schemes of interior decoration, such as Garton on the Wolds (Yorkshire East Riding) or Ashley (Northamptonshire). In the chancel at Ashley there is a broad band of haloed figures in arcades, and narrow bands of decorative motifs, with the wall between lined out as several courses of 'stonework' with rosettes, as described above; the window embrasures are decorated with plant scrolls and there is much gilding of crockets around the sedilia and other architectural features. A major figural scene surrounds the head of the east window, and the celure above the altar position is painted and gilded in medieval fashion.

It is still possible to discover substantial remnants of painting in churches, but needless to say their treatment is a specialist technique. The best that the generalist church archaeologist can do is to summon expert help and campaign for the preservation of the paintings.

(c) Glass

With the exception of a few notable examples, such as Fairford (Gloucester-shire), parish churches do not possess very much glass earlier that the 19th century. Although it is clear both from documentary sources and from excavations at Monkwearmouth/Jarrow (Tyne & Wear) and Glastonbury (Somerset) that coloured window glass was being produced from the early part of the Christian Saxon period, it is rare for a parish church to retain any glass earlier than the 13th century, and usually it is not in its original position. Typically, one finds surviving fragments of medieval and later glass incorporated into new glazing schemes dating from a Victorian restoration. In many cases the new glass has been very skilfully matched to the old, and although modern glass is not often mistaken for medieval or 17th/18th-century work it is quite easy to overlook pieces of old glass in their present setting. The condition of the glass is quite a good guide, however, and where ancient glass has not been the subject of modern conservation techniques there is often a tell-tale patina on the external surface which contrasts quite strongly with the 'clean' appearance of more recent material surrounding it. Medieval glass can be found in unexpected places, such the recently-discovered crypt under the north porch at Fotheringhay (Northamptonshire). Much of the under-ground chamber had been filled with building debris, which on excavation proved to contain considerable fragments of the extensive medieval glazing scheme which had survived into the 18th century. The quest for surviving pieces of old glass should not lead one to overlook the huge quantities of Victorian glass, which tends to be ignored simply because there is such a large amount of it. Much of it, though perhaps not always to the modern taste, is of the greatest interest, for example the windows of the church at Wymeswold (Leicestershire), designed by A W N Pugin – though based on medieval models – for the restoration of the church which he undertook in the late 1840s. From the later 19th century the work of the Pre-Raphaelites is noteworthy, some of it in unlikely locations like the Classical church, probably by Wren, at Ingestre (Staffordshire) or the Baroque Anglican cathedral, designed by Thomas Archer, in Birmingham. In both of these examples the glass is by Burne-Jones. More conventionally, good Victorian glass is found in Victorian churches; of the many examples that could be chosen St Michael's, Brighton, illustrates the work of William Morris's firm (see front cover illustration), which also made the glass for Middleton Cheney (Northamptonshire), where many of the PRB are represented as designers: Burne-Jones, Ford Madox Brown, Philip Webb, Simeon Solomon and Morris himself. What can be seen in a relatively small area is shown by an excellent recent publication on stained glass in Rutland (Sharpling 1997).

It is not possible here to describe the subject matter represented in pictorial windows, and more specialist literature should be sought for an introduction to the multitude of saints, bishops, kings and other worthies who inhabited medieval windows, often under typical architectural canopies and accompanied by donor figures. A wide variety of background and border patterns survives as fragments, as does much heraldic glass (popular also in the post-Reformation period).

Liturgical furniture

Both the structural layout and the design and placing of the furnishings of a place of worship are conditioned by the form of divine service practised by the people responsible for building it. Even within the Christian faith this can vary enormously. For example, the simplicity and informality of the Quaker meeting, devoid of set ritual and prescribed formulae, make few special demands in terms of structure and permanent furnishing, so that the meeting room is scarcely – if at all – distinguishable from a secular room designed to accommodate a similar number of people for general social purposes (as opposed to special-function public rooms, such as theatres). In contrast with this, the High Anglican or Roman Catholic forms of worship, with their developed ceremonial, require both specialist structures and specialist fittings, so that the chancel, and to some extent the other parts, of the church cannot possibly be confused with any other kind of building.

In Britain it is undoubtedly true that the Anglican and other churches, which have inherited a medieval structure originally arranged to accommodate a form of the Roman rite, offer the greatest opportunity for archaeological investigation and a range of potential evidence for changes in liturgical practice both before and after the Reformation, sometimes covering a period of 1000 years or more. The archaeological interest in such buildings and their fittings is self-evident, but it should not be allowed to obscure the importance of more recent structures and their internal arrangements. Though the aspect of development over time is less significant in these cases, the extent to which structures and furnishings are conditioned by liturgical practices is still an observable phenomenon.

In the present context it is impossible – and would, in any case, be inappropriate – to embark on a comparative study of liturgical forms. It is however central to the purposes of this book to give some examples of the way in which liturgical considerations determine what might be called the 'archaeology of furnishings and fittings'. The words 'liturgy' and 'liturgical' should not be taken too literally. A religious group which does not use a missal or a prayer-book, or their equivalent, may nevertheless have developed patterns of worship that are as firmly established as prescribed liturgies, and their effect on the buildings and their contents are as fundamental as, say, the Mass on a Roman

Catholic church. In this sense it is just as appropriate to refer to a Nonconformist 'liturgy' as to an Anglican one.

A convenient, as well as a logical, starting point for a discussion of liturgical matters is the rite of initiation: baptism, in many Christian churches. To the parishioner and the casual visitor alike, the font is a familiar feature in Anglican churches. Its traditional position was close to the main entrance, symbolising the notion that entry to the Church could be achieved only by way of baptism. In the early days of Christianity, the font or its equivalent was housed in a room outside the church proper, sometimes indeed in a separate building, the baptistery. At this stage a larger vessel than a font was used at ground level or below, which was appropriate for the immersion or affusion of adults. The later font developed with the increasing tendency toward infant baptism and with the change to aspersion as the means of administering the rite. In more recent times the Baptists in particular have revived the concept of adult baptism by total immersion. This requires an arrangement rather like a miniature swimming pool, of sufficient size to accommodate both a full-sized adult, prone below the surface of the water, and the minister who performs the ceremony. Unlike the Early Christians, however, the Baptists regard the rite as a central part of normal worship, so the baptistery is in a prominent position in the body of the church, typically below the boarding of a rostrum immediately in front of the congregation.

For most of the time the baptistery is covered, and the platform above it houses the wooden communion table and chairs for the elders or deacons – lay people who assist the minister on those occasions (rare by modern Anglican standards) when Holy Communion is celebrated. The stone altar of Catholic tradition is totally foreign to most Nonconformist places of worship. Above and behind the rostrum, in a prominent, high and central position, is the pulpit, from which worship is conducted and the Word is read and preached. Not since the Tractarian reforms of the 19th century has this been the normal position for the Anglican pulpit, which is typically to one side at the east end of the nave. But in some places, such as King's Norton (Leicestershire), an earlier arrangement has survived (Fig 18). The emphasis of Anglican worship in the 18th century was often close to that of the Nonconformists: Communion was celebrated infrequently, and the King's Norton altar is small and discreetly hidden away behind the prominent central pulpit. From this the Word was preached from the top level, and read from the Bible at intermediate level; as in most Nonconformist churches and chapels this was the focal point in regular worship.

Music forms an important part of many liturgies, but emphases vary and so too do the furnishings associated with it. In some Nonconformist churches and chapels there is a gallery for organ and choir at the end of the worship area, facing the congregation, above and behind the pulpit. This convenient and potentially impressive arrangement is not possible in the medieval buildings inherited by the Church of England. In many cases the organ has to be tucked away in a corner, which is often practically and acoustically unsatisfactory. The

Fig 18   St John Baptist, King's Norton, Leicestershire: view of furnishings from west
(© Crown Copyright; RCHME)

surpliced choir, introduced into parish churches in the 19th century, often sits
in front of the congregation in the medieval chancel; constrained by Victorian
or earlier choirstalls and sometimes isolated by a screen across the chancel

arch, it does not have the same relationship with the congregation as its Nonconformist counterpart. A raised choir at the east end, facing the people, is unthinkable in an ancient Anglican church unless – as is now frequently the case – its altar is moved from the traditional position under the east window to one in the nave, in front of the chancel arch. Many churches still retain the furniture which was common until the middle of the 19th century: a gallery at the west end, ie *behind* the congregation. Here, before organs became an almost universal feature, the village band would provide the music. In some cases the organs that superseded these bands were also accommodated on the west gallery, an arrangement which is still common in Protestant parts of Europe. At Ashby St Ledgers (Northamptonshire) there is an interesting survival in the parish church: at the west end of the south aisle is a raised platform with sloping desks for musicians or singers.

In Roman Catholic and post-Tractarian Anglican rites the altar is the most important piece of liturgical furniture. Before the Reformation it was customary for even quite small churches to have a number of altars and the positions of many of them can be deduced from the tell-tale features surviving in the fabric, usually in side aisles and transepts, or in the main nave walls of aisleless buildings. The classic indicator is the piscina: in the case of Gaddesby it not only identifies a medieval altar position, but provides a vital clue to the analysis of the whole building (see below pp 55–7). Since the purpose of a piscina is to receive the water from the priest's ceremonial ablutions during the Mass, its position was necessarily near to the altar, though in some large churches piscinas were also provided in a vestry or sacristy. In a few cases subsidiary altar positions may also be identified by surviving reredos panels in transept or aisle east walls or by sedilia, the built-in stalls used by the officiating clergy at the Mass. Sedilia, typically in groups of three, most commonly occur in the chancel south wall, and there is usually a piscina associated with them. These features were provided for the service of the principal altar, and their position towards the east end of the chancel implies that the altar was directly beneath or quite close to the east window by the later Middle Ages. Other evidence for the altar position, such as squints, suggests that in some cases or at some times the high altar may have been rather further forward in the chancel, and it appears from excavation that in the early Middle Ages it may have been only just beyond the chancel arch, or indeed in the nave of the church, a position to which it has returned in much modern Anglican and Roman Catholic practice. There is, however, a great deal of uncertainty about this matter, and the systematic recording of liturgical fittings has an important part to play in the resolution of the various problems.

For public use
Relatively few items of furniture are devoted to the convenience of the worshippers or other members of the public using the building. The main one worthy of consideration is seating. Fixed wooden seating in churches seems to

be a late medieval development. It is commonly stated that before this people generally stood throughout services, though it is, in theory, possible that loose benches were used and that people of substance had individual chairs or folding stools. Neither of those would leave any archaeological evidence, and, in particular, the benches themselves are unlikely to have survived. What have survived are numerous masonry benches against the outside walls of naves or side aisles, and in some cases against internal partition walls, as at Gaddesby (Leicestershire). They are also known from excavation, for example at St Mary in Tanner Street, Winchester (Hampshire), where low rubble benches with mortared upper surfaces ran round all three walls of the nave and returned at the east end along the chancel screen. This feature was not later than 14th-century, but in most cases it is not possible to determine the date of such benches. Their purpose was to accommodate worshippers for whom standing throughout the Mass was either impossible or undesirable: the aged, the infirm and the pregnant.

When wooden seating was introduced, it normally took the form of open benches set across the axis of the church and supported on sleeper beams. The vertical timber panels forming the ends of the benches were usually carved, the simplest ones with plain tracery or heraldic designs and the more elaborate with more ambitious designs surmounted by the well-known 'poppy head' finials in high relief and sometimes by carving in the round (eg animals) on the arm rests. Even where the medieval seating scheme has been destroyed, which is the case in most churches, some of the bench ends are likely to have survived and to have been incorporated into later furniture.

After the Reformation the design of benches began to include doors at the ends, so that they became completely enclosed. With the increased importance of the sermon in 18th-century worship the previously regimented layout of benches gave way to a more practical arrangement in which seats in different parts of the building were positioned so that their occupants could face the pulpit, which might be half-way along one of the side walls. In some parts of the church benches might develop into larger enclosed areas with seats all round the interior. At this period the allocation of 'pews' to families or individuals became a matter of some importance, and in some cases people staked their claim by putting their name, or that of their property, on the panelling of their seat. At Astbury (Cheshire) personal names are carved on the woodwork, and at West Grinstead (W Sussex) the names of the farms in the parish are painted on the backs of the benches. Meanwhile, seating in Nonconformist chapels developed along similar lines, though the adoption of building plans different from the traditional medieval church led to alternative arrangements of the furnishings. For example, open-plan buildings like the former Wesleyan chapel in Brixworth (Northamptonshire; now a private house), with its pulpit in one corner, lent themselves to concentric arrangements. This sort of seating plan was also appropriate to some purpose-built post-Reformation Anglican churches, eg All Saints', Newcastle upon Tyne.

The large, elaborate family pew, owned, provided and exclusively used by a well-to-do local family, is a feature of the Anglican parish church in the 17th and 18th centuries. These were more elaborate than the larger areas of fixed seating just described. They were often free-standing, independent structures, sometimes subdivided internally into separate 'rooms', which considerably reduced the space available within the church for public use. In this and other respects they were the Protestant equivalent of the chantry chapels of pre-Reformation times, which were privately endowed and often took up as much as half of a side aisle, or a complete transept. The chapels have almost entirely disappeared, as a result of the dismantling of the chantry system in 1547, but where they were formed by the screening-off of parts of the church itself, it is still possible to see the marks in the masonry where timbers were inserted to hold the panelling (as for example at Gaddesby, see below pp 55–8). In some rare cases free-standing chantry chapels still survive; at Lavenham (Suffolk) there are two, made of timber posts and panels, and elaborately carved, while at Boxgrove Priory (W Sussex) there is a no less elaborate structure of masonry and stucco, built through an arch between the former choir and its south aisle.

Returning to the public seating, the Victorian restorers of Anglican churches tended to sweep away 17th- and 18th-century schemes in favour of open benches of medieval type. However, they continued the post-medieval tendency to fill the body of the church with furniture, which was not entirely convenient for some of the non-liturgical uses to which churches had traditionally been put. The 19th-century attitude was that most of the activities were not appropriate to the church, which should be reserved for worship. This had not been the view in the Middle Ages, and all sorts of activities from public meetings to play-acting had taken place in church. For some of these it was convenient to have fixed seating in the nave, but for others it was not. The jollifications that followed the annual audit of the churchwardens' accounts and the stalls associated with a saint's day fair both needed space, and accounts of hogsheads of ale set up in the church imply a certain amount of room not occupied by fixed furniture. The apparatus required for the wide variety of secular activities in church – cradles for beer barrels, actors' props, and so on – was largely impermanent, and those uses have left little trace in the furnishings and fittings of most churches. In some cases, however, the furniture of the parish library survives, occasionally still with its chained books, and there is sometimes evidence for the schools which were frequently kept in church, for example the master's desk at Melton Mowbray (Leicestershire). Other parish activities are represented by such things as fire engines or fire buckets and collections of armour, but those belong to the contents rather than to the furnishings of the church.

An activity which has had a significant and permanent impact on the fabric of many Anglican churches is bell-ringing. There is documentary evidence for the existence of bells and archaeological evidence for the casting of them (usually inside the church itself) from well before the Norman Conquest. By the end of the Middle Ages bells were beginning to proliferate and a surprising number survive from this period in parish churches. After the Reformation even quite small churches had several bells, the bell-wheel was introduced, and change-ringing developed. Bell-ringing for its own sake has become a largely secular pastime seemingly quite divorced, in many cases, from the primary purpose of the churches which house the bells. It is a far cry from the single bell of the Middle Ages, which summoned people to Mass; not all churches had even that bare minimum, since the possession of a bell had to do with status in the ecclesiastical hierarchy and required legal permission. The bells themselves, both medieval and modern, are archaeological artefacts in their own right, with a recognised typology; many have inscriptions, and some are dated. The frames in which they are hung are also of interest, even though the old ones have often been replaced in the interests of stability, by cast iron from the 19th century onward and, more recently, by concrete ring beams. Earlier wooden frames still exist in some places, however. Some are dated, which not only helps in the establishment of a typology for the frames themselves but also casts light on carpentry techniques in general. Care must be taken, however, not to be misled by reused timbers; the recycling tradition was active in belfries just as it was in roof structures.

Further reading
Addleshaw & Etchells 1948; Bond 1908, etc; CBA 1985; Caiger-Smith 1963; Cox 1922; Cox & Harvey 1907; Davies 1968; NADFAS 1989; Randall 1980; Sharpling 1997.

Case Study II

The Leicestershire example presented here illustrates the way in which it is possible to reconstruct the internal arrangement of a church in the late Middle Ages. This, together with a small amount of fabric analysis, makes it possible to draw some conclusions about how a church was used in the 14th century.

St Luke, Gaddesby, Leicestershire
As the published plan shows (Fig 19), the scale of Gaddesby church belies its original status of dependent chapelry in the great soke of Rothley, a pre-Conquest estate with tentacles throughout north and east Leicestershire. No doubt because of the extent of the soke and their distance from the mother church at Rothley (where there was a priest at Domesday and where a carved Anglo-Saxon cross-shaft survives), the chapels of the dependencies tended to develop as though they were parish churches in their own right. Gaddesby is a notable example, with its five-bay nave (whose original fabric is 12th century or earlier), its substantial west tower, its side aisles clasping the tower and its long 15th-century chancel.

Considerable evidence survives of the way in which the large area of the

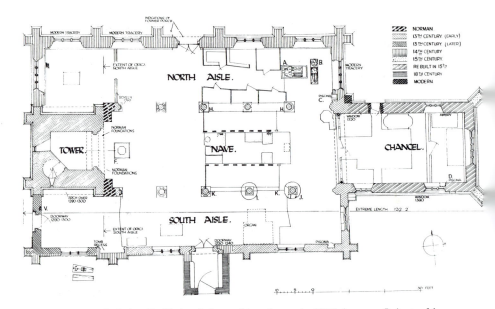

Fig 19   St Luke, Gaddesby, Leicestershire: plan as in 1925 (courtesy Leicestershire Archaeological and Historical Society)

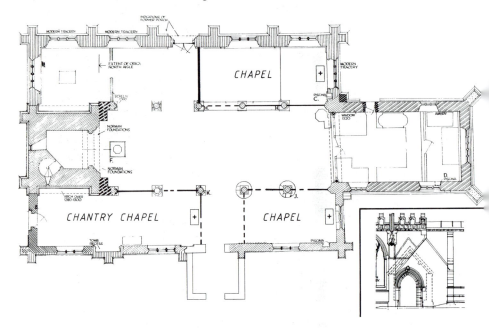

Fig 20   St Luke, Gaddesby: reconstructed late medieval plan. (The inset shows part of Herbert's south elevation drawing, which gives the evidence for the original position of the porch)

body of the church was subdivided in late medieval times. On the north side a sleeper wall still stands to a considerable height (about 0.70m) between the piers of the third and fourth bays of the nave arcade. It is not clear whether this is a remnant of the original north wall before the insertion of the arcade. The division between the nave and the north aisle was carried up further in timber, though it is not possible to deduce whether this was in the form of a full partition or of an openwork screen. The top of the divider seems to have been at the level of the arcade capitals, some of which have been cut into to form a shallow mortise for the top rail. The screened-off part of the north aisle extended three bays from the east end. On the north side of the third pier base a huge, vertical slot was cut, apparently to accommodate the lower part of a heavy screen (approximately 180mm wide) running across the aisle just to the east of the north door. The area of the aisle thus enclosed was without doubt a self-contained chapel. The former presence of an altar, on the site of or just to the east of the monument marked 'B' on the plan (since removed to a position against the north wall), is confirmed by the piscina preserved in the east wall, to the south of the window, and by the image brackets which survive on either side of the same window. The floor of the easternmost bay of the chapel is

Fig 21   St Luke, Gaddesby: details of south-west and north-east respond capitals of nave arcades

55

slightly raised, indicating the extent of the sanctuary. The assumption that this was the late medieval arrangement is confirmed by the fact that the horizontal moulding at sill level in the aisle north wall (which is 14th-century or earlier) rises by a corresponding amount at the junction of the western part of the chapel and the altar bay. The two 'public' bays were furnished with longitudinal bench seating; the masonry bench structures survive along the aisle wall to the north and the sleeper wall to the south.

There is similar evidence for a corresponding enclosed chapel at the east end of the south aisle. There is a piscina in the south wall and an image bracket to the south of the east window; traces of its companion on the north side are visible in certain lighting conditions. The central part of the window (approximately half of the total width) is dropped to form a half-height niche, which originally held either a statue of the patron saint of the altar or the altar cross, which commonly stood behind, rather than on, the altar. Interference with the masonry of the south arcade suggests screens of the kind adduced for the north-east chapel. The south-east chapel can have been only two bays long, as will become apparent below. However, there is no evidence on the south side of the second pier from the east for the screen that must have existed in this position. Any evidence in the corresponding part of the south wall of the aisle is unfortunately obscured by the organ.

The remainder of the south aisle provides the most illuminating and exciting evidence for the medieval ordering of the church. The marks in the masonry of the screens fitted into the arcade arches are particularly clear (Fig 21). There is also evidence on the south face of the second pier from the west for a similar screen running across the south aisle. With the church in its present form it would appear that this screen would have met the line of the south wall roughly in the middle of the south door, which is plainly ridiculous. It is evident, however, that the doorway is not in its original position, even though there are no convincing marks of insertion in the surrounding masonry as seen from inside the church. From the outside, though, it is clear that the south *porch* has been moved to the west (Fig 20 inset). Two phases of porch preceding the present 18th-century structure are demonstrated by classic 'fossilised' roof-lines, the first a raised stone weathering strip, and the second a groove cut in the masonry to take lead flashing. If the porch were to be reconstructed in the position indicated by the projecting weathering, its west wall would interfere with the fabric of the south door in its present position. The door must therefore also have been moved from a position further to the east. Its centre was originally some 1.2m east of the apex of the present doorway, whose fabric appears to be of 13th-century date; this masonry is therefore likely to have formed the original doorway. The insertion of the doorway in its present position is confirmed by further evidence inside the south aisle, where the reset masonry can be seen to cut a shallow niche in the south wall just to the west of the entrance.

If the south door were restored to its original place, the north–south screen attached to the second arcade pier from the west would meet solid walling at its south end, as shown in the reconstruction plan (Fig 20). Once again, an area of three bays is defined by closure screens, two bays corresponding with arches of the south arcade and the third with the tower. In an attempt to emphasise the unity of this fairly long, narrow space, a false arch was inserted between the buttresses of the tower. Superficially this appears to continue the line of the south arcade.

Externally this part of the south aisle was very elaborately refaced in the 14th century, and its fabric contrasts strongly with that to the east of the original south porch. The fine grey limestone stands out against the brown ironstone of much of the rest of the church. The buttresses have gables encrusted with carved ornament and were once surmounted by pinnacles rising above the parapet. The parapet itself is covered with low-relief decoration and the merlons have an unusual stepped profile. The west elevation of the aisle and the buttresses at the south-west angle incorporate image niches with rich canopy work. In the end wall this elaborate decoration surrounds a window in the shape of a curved-sided triangle above a somewhat plainer (and probably earlier) door.

What was the purpose of all this enrichment, and indeed of the enclosing of space? Both structural and documentary evidence suggest that it must have been a private chapel. At the east end the partially destroyed niche near the south door must have been more than a mere aumbry. The surviving reveal is provided with a small attached shaft with base and capital, above which the line of an arched head can still be seen. A carved human head, still intact, served as the stop for the hoodmould of this arch. When complete, the feature must have been more than 1m wide. Almost certainly it is a piscina, though the basin and drain-hole cut in the sill, which would have put the identification beyond doubt, are missing. A piscina in this position implies an altar against the putative eastern screen, and thus the use of the area as a chapel. An altar here would have precluded any access to the chapel from the main south entrance, and there may also have been none from the body of the church, because of the screens across the arches of the south arcade. Entry to the chapel was through the door in the west wall, which is a most unusual feature to find in a church aisle. Direct access from the exterior emphasises the private nature of the chapel, which was probably the prerogative of an important local family, one of whose number was buried in the tomb recess that was inserted into the fabric in the 14th century, probably in the course of the external refurbishment described above.

There is documentary evidence for three substantial chantry endowments in the 1320s and 1330s, two of which were made by the same family. The amount of property alienated in these grants suggests that either of the families was prosperous enough to afford the extensive – and doubtless quite expensive – work on the fabric of the south aisle, and it is a reasonable inference that the western part of the aisle served as their chantry chapel. Since, apparently,

Robert de Overton and Robert of Gaddesby (the two grantors mentioned in the documents) were not one and the same person, then there must have been another chantry chapel which was the subject of whichever endowment did not apply in the south aisle. This may have been the eastern part of the north aisle, where the surviving monuments of late 15th-century date suggest continued private use, though the family names of the inscriptions do not have any immediate connection with those of the 14th-century chantry founders. This would leave the two bays at the east end of the south aisle to act as a Lady Chapel, which was *de rigueur* in medieval churches from the 12th century on.

The interior arrangement of Gaddesby church in the 14th century was thus very different from the open plan of today, in which the whole church apart from the chancel is publicly available space. All but one bay of the south aisle was screened off to form chapels, and entry to the church by the south door must have led through a corridor between wooden screens, at the end of which the central arch of the south arcade gave on to the nave. Directly opposite and to the right were the screens enclosing the north-east chapel. There is no structural evidence at the west end of the north aisle, but this too may have been partitioned off, leaving only the nave as the space available for public use, whether liturgical or otherwise. The feeling of being hemmed in would have been increased by the almost complete separation of the chancel from the nave. Up to about the height of the chancel arch capitals there was the usual screen, and above this a solid tympanum made of boards or of lath and plaster, possibly painted, and serving as the background for the great rood or crucifix. Mortise holes in the soffit show where the main vertical members of this tympanum were fitted into the chancel arch. The boards of a tympanum of this kind were discovered during the restoration of the church at Wenhaston (Suffolk) and examples can still be seen in several places, for instance at Ashlehurst (Gloucestershire), where the boards were painted in post-medieval times with the Royal Arms.

Note: The basic literature on Gaddesby is a joint article by Albert Herbert and G F Farnham in the *Transactions of the Leicestershire Archaeological Society* **13** (1923–24), 246–65. Herbert's measured drawings accompany this account: his plate I is reproduced here as Figure 19 and part of his plate II provides the inset for Figure 20. The chantry endowments are published in an appendix on pp 266–8.

Chapter 4: Documentary Evidence

This introduction to the written sources is confined almost entirely to the records of the Church of England. This is no arbitrary decision based on prejudice or the author's convenience; there are several cogent reasons why it should be so. First, the buildings of the Church of England have been subject to more intense use over a far longer period than those of any other denomination, and thus stand in far greater need of elucidation by whatever means, including reference to the documents. Second, the Church of England inherited at the Reformation the established hierarchical system of the Roman Catholic church with its organisation, legal structure and pattern of control based on the dioceses and their sub-divisions. This was accompanied by a semi-centralised system of record-keeping, so that there exists, potentially, a fairly consistent range of documents, and the survival rate for some classes of material has been relatively high. Third, some Anglican records at parish level, in particular the registers of baptisms, marriages and burials, have also been secular legal documents, which has been a powerful restraint on their destruction. The habit of retaining and preserving registers has tended to rub off on other parish documents, though stories of the wholesale destruction of records after the death of an incumbent are all too common.

This is not to imply that the records of Nonconformist and other Christian groups are not worthy of study, but in most cases there is no centralised organisation or control and therefore no easily identifiable set of documents at other than local community level. Amongst the longer-established Nonconformist churches and chapels there are local collections of records comparable with those of Anglican parishes. The minutes of deacons', elders', or management committees' meetings are the equivalent of Anglican vestry or Parochial Church Council records; the annual chapel accounts are the counterpart of Anglican churchwardens' accounts; and the fabric committee's correspondence with its architect, and his drawings and specifications, are the same whatever the denomination. Nonconformist records are mentioned briefly in *Hallelujah!* (CBA 1985, 43–5). Other Christian groups, from Greek Orthodox to Caribbean, as well as non-Christian faiths, are less straightforward. In practice, however, many of them have taken over redundant Anglican or Nonconformist places of worship, so that much of the information about the history of these buildings has to be sought in the records, if any survive, of the previous users.

Church of England records

For practical purposes the highest level of Anglican records is that of *diocesan* or *episcopal records*. Diocesan bishops transact a great deal of business and only a small part of it refers to the fabric of individual churches. There is the occasional mention of such matters in *bishops' registers*, but it can be a laborious task to find the information referring to a particular church unless the registers are published with an index or there is a place-name index at the record office where the unpublished volumes are kept. Much more easily identified and usually much more informative are *faculties*, which can be found singly or copied up into *faculty registers*. These are legal documents giving the bishop's permission for work to be carried out on the fabric or furniture of a parish church or chapel. They are often accompanied by a specification and plan of the proposed work. Although the faculty system has been in existence for a long time it has been applied consistently only over the last 150 years or so. Even during this period it should not be assumed that parishes always applied for a faculty when they carried out work on the church. Bishops were also involved in visiting the parishes in their dioceses, as were the archdeacons in their areas of responsibility. The state of the church fabric was enquired into, among other things, and a note of any action required was entered in the *visitation book*. Subsequent visitation documents often reveal that the work had been carried out, and sometimes the total sum expended on it is recorded, so that there is a possibility of assessing the actual extent of what was done. Associated material includes the *presentments*, which contained the evidence submitted to the bishop or archdeacon by the incumbent or the churchwardens, and the *acts* of the *courts*, to which cases arising from a visitation were brought. Slightly more informative are *church inspection* or *survey books*, because they record more specific enquiries than the visitation books.

With the exception of the faculties, most of the documents at episcopal or archidiaconal level offer only brief and general information. For more detail one must turn to the parish records. It should be said straight away that the commonest of these, the *registers of baptisms, marriages and burials*, are least likely to be informative. Not only do they have a clearly defined purpose, which has no connection with the church fabric, but since 1813 they have been printed with a prescribed format for each entry, and this has afforded little space and no encouragement for the writing of miscellaneous notes. Such memoranda were a common feature of the earlier registers, especially where baptisms, marriages and burials were all entered in the same book, but in three separate lists. This was a recipe for odd blank pages, which invited all kinds of unofficial use, ranging from mere doodles to serious records of parish events. Among those are sometimes references to the repair or restoration of the church, or to other events affecting the fabric, such as fire, storm or earthquake. There is an interesting memorandum buried deep in the 18th-century register at Carlton, a chapelry of Market Bosworth (Leicestershire). In 1764 the children born in the village had to be taken to other places for baptism, because the chapel at Carlton was in such disrepair as to be unusable. The flyleaves of 18th-century and earlier registers were also used to record *briefs*, which were officially authorised collections made from place to place in favour of some disaster fund. Sometimes the object of the collection was a church which had been damaged, for example All Saints', Northampton, destroyed in the town fire in 1675, or St Mary's, Warwick, which suffered a similar fate in 1694. In some cases the note in the register of parish *x* that money was collected is the only record of work being contemplated on the church of parish *y*.

The information in the parish registers, then, is only incidental and often very brief. For more detail one should turn to the parish copies of *any faculties* issued by the bishop or his representative. These have already been discussed (see p 60). The decision to apply for a faculty or to do whatever work was envisaged is often recorded in the *vestry* (since 1921 *PCC) minutes.* Some of these go into great detail about contracts and consider the merits of competing tenders for the work. The other official parish document that frequently contains information about the church fabric is the *churchwardens' accounts.* If purchases of large quantities of building materials are entered in the accounts, then work may be taking place on the church, though such entries may equally refer to the building of parish rooms or the reconstruction of the churchyard wall: accounts do not often specify what the materials were bought for.

The parish records may also include *correspondence* between the incumbent and the patron, who formerly had sole responsibility for the upkeep of the chancel, and who might also be persuaded to contribute to the restoration or maintenance of the rest of the building. Sometimes the work would be commissioned by the parish, who then sent the bill to the patron, and sometimes the patron would make the arrangements himself. In this case the only record of the transaction would be in the patron's *private or estate papers.* Since he often lived at a distance from the parish, these documents may not form part of the local archive, and since 'he' was often a corporate body (eg an Oxbridge college after the Reformation, or a monastery before it) the relevant papers may form part of a rather special collection of documents. For example, the total rebuilding of the chancel of St Mary, Adderbury (Oxfordshire), between 1408 and 1419 is recorded in the archive of New College, Oxford. Fortunately, in this case the accounts have been published (Hobson 1926) and are easily available for consultation. It is worth noting that, in the case of private chapels, this is likely to be the only kind of documentary evidence available for either the chancel or the nave. An example of this is the record of expenditure on the new building in the grounds of Staunton Harold Hall (Leicestershire) in the 1660s. The payments are scattered among the general items of estate expenditure in the Shirley family papers, now lodged in the Warwickshire Record Office.

Returning to parish records, there is often quite voluminous correspondence between the incumbent or churchwardens and their architects and contractors. This can include descriptions of the building and the state of the fabric, as well as details of work to be undertaken or already carried out. From the architects' side there may be *specifications, plans* and other *drawings.* Good specifications can give an accurate picture of the work which the architect intended to carry out, but it should not be assumed that this is what was actually done. A classic case is the reordering of Repton church (Derbyshire) in 1792. A faculty issued in the previous year had included a detailed specification for a complete new scheme of enclosed seats surrounding a central three-decker pulpit, but there was no mention of the fact that, to make the preacher visible from the sittings in the transept, considerable amounts of the nave walls would have to be removed to make two arches on either side (or rather to unblock already existing arches). Similarly, at Appleby Magna (Leicestershire) there is a most detailed specification attached to a faculty of 1827, which includes the erection of a west gallery. This gallery was clearly going to interfere with the access to the church through opposed doorways towards the west end of the aisle walls, but the specification allows only for the blocking of the north door. In the event, both doorways were blocked up, porches on both sides of the church were removed, and windows and flanking buttresses, to match those existing, were built in the affected bays of the aisle walls. None of this extra work was mentioned in the specification or indeed in any other document so far discovered, including the plan accompanying the faculty. This and the other architect's drawings are a model of draughtsmanship, and very informative about the church in the early 19th century. Many parishes have drawings of this sort among their records, though in some cases the knowledge to be gained is limited by a lack of plans and elevations showing the building as it was before work began.

What ultimately is needed is a record of work completed. This can be afforded by contractors' and tradesmen's bills, which are often not individually represented in the churchwardens' accounts. Such bills may specify the various items of expenditure, and, if so, they are a very good guide to what has actually been done. Even an account rendered 'To work on the church as per estimate' is useful, because it indicates that what was planned was in fact carried out, though if the *estimate* does not survive, other means have to be found of defining what the job was. In the case of major restorations a special fund was often set up, with a final *report and account* presented on completion to a public meeting and to individual subscribers and benefactors. In the 19th century these were often printed documents and they sometimes gave details of the restoration work, though these are most likely to have been included in a prospectus used initially to launch an appeal for funds.

In some parish collections there are *illustrations* of various sorts showing part of the church – sketches, watercolours, photographs, picture postcards. There is a chance that these will give information on an earlier state of the fabric or its furnishings, but a difficulty with this kind of material is that it is rarely dated, and one often has to use the church to explain the picture rather than the other way round.

Other original documents and secondary sources

In addition to the documents belonging to one or another department of the Anglican church, there is a great deal of material, largely pictorial, in public or private ownership. Examples of material publicly available are the photographic collection at the National Buildings Record (the Church of England also has a collection of photographs housed at the Council for the Care of Churches) and the numerous paintings and drawings in the local collections of art galleries and museums up and down the country. It may be more profitable to consult the special collections, such as the Sussex Archaeological Society's Sharpe collection of watercolours and drawings, which show Sussex churches as they were between 1797 and 1809 (the Society published a useful catalogue in 1979); or the Uppingham School collection of similar pictures dating from the 1830s (published in 1983 as *Rutland churches before Restoration);* or the collection of drawings by Sir J G Wilkinson from Calke Abbey, now in the Bodleian Library, which show churches in various parts of the country in their pre-restoration state.

Other illustrations occur in printed form, for example those of the 18th-century antiquary William Stukeley or the engravings of the brothers Buck or the hand-coloured drawings of David and Samuel Lysons. The work of lesser-known engravers appears in many of the early county histories (see Figs 1 and 22a). Such *printed books* can also give important factual information about churches and their furnishings. For example, Bigsby's *Description of Repton* (1854) gives an account of the breaching of the nave walls of St Wystan's church, which was so blatantly omitted from the terms of the 1791 faculty (see above, p 62). Less helpful are the often purely descriptive and quite subjective articles and notes in historical and archaeological *journals,* both national and local, though the early ones may refer to features which have since disappeared. In this connection early county *directories* are sometimes informative, though the entries are necessarily brief. A useful source for restoration and new church building in the 19th century is the local *newspaper.* Reports of services at the dedication or re-opening were often padded out with a description of the church and details of the restoration which were frequently culled from the appeal literature. These and other 'secular' sources refer to Nonconformist as well as to Anglican places of worship. In the case of newspapers, the emphasis tended to reflect their political allegiance: the conservative press concentrated on the affairs of the established Church, while the more radical papers gave more coverage to the Nonconformists.

A further source of information on Anglican churches before restoration is the 'Church notes' by Sir Stephen Glynne, a 19th-century antiquarian who travelled much of the country recording his observations church by church. His notes form part of the collection of St Deiniol's Library at Hawarden, near Chester; for some parts of the country edited versions have been published, either as substantial articles in antiquarian journals or as volumes in record society series. A few county record offices have copies of the entries relevant to their locality.

Further reading
Cox 1913; Humphrey 1981; Owen 1970; introduction to Parsons 1984.

Case Study III

To illustrate the range of documents and the information which can be obtained from them the records of two parishes collected for the *Bibliography of Leicestershire Churches* have been chosen. The material presented here has not so far been published in the *Bibliography*, with the exception of the newspaper accounts. The examples have been selected to show how different parish archives can be one from another, both in their size and in the kinds of information that they yield. What follows is a pair of 'thumb-nail sketches', and neither claims to give a full account either of the documents available or of the history of the church concerned.

(a) Melton Mowbray, Leicestershire

St Mary's, Melton Mowbray, is a large, aisled, cruciform church of some pretension in a prosperous east Leicestershire market town. It is very well documented at all levels – episcopal, archidiaconal and parochial. The church is first mentioned by implication in *Domesday Book* (1086), which records two priests and an extensive 'family' of dependencies, several of which are still chapelries of Melton today. At this stage the church must have been a still surviving pre-Conquest minster. The present fabric has some Norman masonry in the crossing tower, and is likely to have been cruciform in the 12th century, if not before. This is one of the plan forms appropriate to an ancient minster.

From the 13th century on, a series of mentions in the bishops' registers give little precise information about the church fabric but in the 16th century there is an increasing amount of documentary evidence. This begins with information in the fabric of the church itself: the building or rebuilding of the vestry on the north side of the chancel in 1532 is recorded by a relief inscription on one of the stone ashlars in its east wall. Shortly after this, there is, in the churchwardens' accounts, an almost blow-by-blow description of the effects of the Reformation and its aftermath on the furnishings of the church. In 1549, during the reign of Edward VI, the wardens paid 20*d* for taking down the (masonry) high altar and another altar in the vestry, and spent 4*s* 1*d* on making a (wooden) communion table 'and other things in the church'. A series of entries in 1553 shows the effect of Queen Mary's putting the clock back: the replacement of the high altar, including the carriage of stones, lime and sand, cost a total of 7*s* 6*d*. This work was undone again under Elizabeth I at a cost of 2*s* 2*d* in 1559, and the communion table was mended so that it could be brought back into use. Meanwhile the rood and roodloft, which appear to have survived the first wave of Protestantism, had been repaired in 1558, but were removed in 1561.

Sundry repairs and the construction of seats are recorded in the later 16th century and after until, in 1690, a faculty gave authority to demolish the ruinous chapel of ease at Eye Kettleby (a deserted village) to provide building materials for the repair of the parish church. Visitation records indicate maintenance and repair work continuing through the 18th century, but do not include an apparent restoration in the early 1740s, in the course of which the seating was rationalised, and an imposing pulpit introduced. Evidence for this comes from the churchwardens' accounts. A succession of documents in the parish archive refers to galleries in the church, which were apparently first built in 1812, replaced by faculty in 1846 and altered again in 1858. Meanwhile GG Scott had written a report on the condition of the fabric and suggested improvements costing an estimated £3925. In 1861 a similar report was received from the architect William Slater with an estimate for proposed work of £7000. However, a scheme by Scott seems to have been carried out in 1868; the faculty for this, dated 14 October 1867, survives in two copies, one in the bishop's and the other in the parish records. In the same year the bishop's visitation papers note that the church was undergoing repair, and this appears to have been the case continually until the early years of the present century. Further work in the 20th century is indicated by several faculties: a new heating system in 1928; the conversion of the south transept into a chapel in 1929, followed by the restoration of the organ, the moving of the font and the erection of new choir stalls; and work on the bells in 1944.

The 19th-century documents are paralleled by extensive reporting in the local press from May 1844 onward. Over the next 30 years or so there were 54 items published in the *Leicester Journal,* 15 in the *Leicester Chronicle,* 40 in the *Stamford Mercury,* and at least one in the *Grantham Journal* (which has not been systematically searched in the course of the bibliography project). This last account, which was published on 12 April 1875, refers to the reseating scheme in Melton church. It was discovered in the form of cuttings in one of the registers of Ashby Folville, a parish several miles from Melton Mowbray.

The overall impression is that this parish church is exceptionally well documented, but with the exception of some of the records dating from the second half of the 19th century, most of the information relates to the furnishings rather than to the fabric of the building.

(b) Snarestone, Leicestershire
St Bartholomew, Snarestone, is, and has always been, a chapelry of Swepstone in west Leicestershire (where, incidentally, there was a priest at Domesday). The status of the chapel, and thus by implication its existence, is first recorded in 1220 in the Matriculus of Hugh de Welles, Bishop of Lincoln. The chapel is further listed in the 1526 subsidy (this, like the Matriculus, has been

Fig 22   St Bartholomew, Snarestone, Leicestershire: (a, above) view from south-west,
c *1800 (after J Nichols,* History and Antiquities of the County of Leicester, **3**, *1804,*
pl cxxxv) (b, below) present-day view from the west

published) but there are otherwise no known medieval references. The form of the medieval chapel is not known and it was mentioned for the first and last time at a visitation in 1743, when the churchwardens stated that its roof was soon to be repaired. Whether this promise was ever carried out is not known. The chapel was replaced by a new brick building in 1752, though no contemporary record of this has survived. The first documentary reference to the rebuilding occurs in the archdeacon's visitation records of 1832, but the information and a brief description had already been published by Nichols in his *History and Antiquities of the County of Leicester* in 1804, accompanied by an engraving which shows a simple, modest, but pleasant and well-proportioned little chapel (see Fig 22a). Early in the 19th century the building was clearly being regarded as too small. In 1818 several estimates were obtained for extending the gallery, and for enlarging and repewing the chapel. Nothing was done, however, until a faculty in November 1834 authorised the removal of the north wall and the extension of the building in that direction by 11ft 3in (*c* 3.43m). At the archdeacon's visitation in August 1835 the cost of this work was recorded as £218. Apart from the obvious practical advantages, its effect was to spoil the symmetry of the chapel, as seen from the outside (Fig 22b), and to produce an unsatisfying box-like interior.

Within 30 years the roof was in need of repair, and references to it recur until the 1930s, when the church finally had a new roof. Shortly after, the old brick floor was replaced in wood block, but without consultation with the Incorporated Church Building Society, which had made a small contribution to the reroofing. As a consequence, ICBS refused to make any further grants.

The Snarestone archive, like the church, is small, and some of the items of information in it are relatively insignificant. The main interest lies in the fact that the effects of the work carried out and documented in 1834–5 can still be seen in the fabric. The records are fairly typical of minor churches in semi-rural locations.

Chapter 5: Recording the Information

Introduction

The case studies in the previous chapters have shown something of the nature and range of the evidence available for studying places of worship. At Bardsey the evidence related to the development of the structure of the church and was largely of a mechanical nature and contained within the fabric itself, while architectural evidence and *in situ* fittings at Gaddesby made possible a reconstruction of the late medieval furnishing scheme; such apparently minor items as slots cut through masonry mouldings proved to be crucial in arriving at a diagnosis. Finally, Melton Mowbray and Snarestone gave an opportunity to demonstrate how documents can both complement the other forms of evidence and provide information on features which no longer exist.

In ideal circumstances all three kinds of evidence may be available to enable the investigator to achieve at least a provisional interpretation. It is essential that, having recognised them, he or she should, as a matter of priority, make an adequate record both of the objective information and of the subjective conclusions that have been arrived at. The urgency of recording is demonstrated by the ephemeral nature of even structural evidence, such as the line of the original porch gable at Bardsey, which has all but disappeared during the lifetime of one scholar (see above, p 33). Similar masonry joints were apparent in the piers on the south side of Brixworth church, Northamptonshire, when the Brixworth Archaeological Research Committee began its work in 1971. Subsequent repointing has obliterated the evidence, but fortunately not before it had been photographed and recorded on elevation drawings. Furnishings and fittings are by nature less permanent and are prone to vanish almost over night in re-ordering schemes or in the course of adapting redundant churches and chapels to new uses, as the Introduction has made clear. It hardly needs saying that the documents are even more vulnerable than the fabric or the furnishings. It is important to record the evidence for other than 'rescue' reasons. It is obviously a waste of time for several investigators to record and interpret the same building on a number of separate occasions, but such duplication is likely to occur unless the first researcher makes a proper record of what he has seen and done and lodges it in an accessible place (which naturally includes publishing it).

There are fortunately plenty of guides to recording techniques which have been published in the last few decades. Several of these deal with vernacular buildings where the problems of access are different from those encountered by the recorder of churches and chapels, particularly medieval ones. Nevertheless, the general approaches to recording are the same, as are the equipment required and the techniques of producing finished illustrations. Here one should mention the CBA's *Recording Old Houses,* by R W MacDowall, and Lance Smith's *Investigating Old Buildings.* The latter has most useful sections on drawing and on researching the background to buildings being surveyed; like most books in this category it has plenty of examples of working and finished drawings, which are well worth studying. A general but very instructive book is RCHME's *Photographing Historic Buildings,* by Terry Buchanan. More particularly on places of worship, CBA has also published *Hallelujah!: recording chapels and meeting places* and *Recording a Church: an illustrated glossary* (Cocke *et al* 1996). The first of these deals with the architecture, furnishings and documents of Nonconformist chapels, and the *Glossary* is concerned with the terminology used to describe the parts of an Anglican parish church. The NADFAS guide, *Inside Churches* (NADFAS 1989), is a much more detailed explanation of the terms which apply to furnishings and fittings, and has specimen descriptions of a large number of subjects together with many line illustrations. The CBA Handbook *Recording Worked Stones,* although a guide to the recording of individual architectural fragments, is very helpful when it comes to drawing detail in standing buildings. Parsons and Brooke (1994) deal with church recording in the context of buildings archaeology generally; they place more emphasis than is possible here on major projects and issues of organisation and funding of church survey work. Finally, since the first edition of this handbook was published, a comprehensive book on surveying historic buildings has appeared. Swallow *et al* (1993) is comprehensive, although to the amateur investigator it may seem a little over-technical. However, the authors' straightforward style of writing, the helpful sub-headings and the many clear illustrations make the book much more accessible than would appear at first sight. On the other hand, there is little specifically on recording places of worship as opposed to historic buildings generally, and most of the examples are of houses, offices, factories, and so on.

The purpose of the record

What form the recording should take depends on the purpose for which the record is required. For a basic listing in a Sites and Monuments Record or for an entry in the 'Year's Work' section of an archaeological journal, a simple outline plan and a brief verbal description may be all that is needed. For a planning or faculty application slightly more elaborate scale plans and elevations, with details of features to be altered, would be needed in most cases, but an archaeologist might wish an even more detailed record to be kept where alteration is proposed; good photographs would also be desirable. In the case of buildings threatened with demolition a complete systematic survey is called for, with a full set of scale drawings (plans at more than one level, all elevations, interior and exterior) and a comprehensive set of photographs. If a building, whether under threat or not, has been the subject of archaeological or art-historical research, then photographs and scale drawings of relevant details and reconstruction diagrams (restored plan, perspective, isometric, cutaway, etc) should be added, and in some cases full stone-by-stone elevation drawings may be appropriate. Such a high level of recording is clearly beyond the resources and capabilities of most individual investigators or small amateur groups, and inappropriate for most practical purposes. The production of a huge portfolio of drawings, photographs and text may indeed be an embarrassment to the museum, archive office or library where the record is to be lodged, and it is worth planning the recording procedure in advance with the keeper of whatever repository is likely to house the archive. It is a waste of time and effort to record beyond the level appropriate to the purpose in hand (except to improve one's own knowledge or technique) or to produce a body of material that is impossible to store. With that proviso, the investigator has the choice of the methods described in the following pages, either singly or in combination.

Since the first edition of this handbook was published, the Royal Commission on the Historical Monuments of England has produced and subsequently revised a brief specification for the use of its own investigators, which also offers guidance to anyone concerned with the recording of historic buildings (RCHME 1996). This sets out in summary form four different levels of recording, with an indication in each case of the circumstances to which it is appropriate. The remainder of the document deals in more detail with the written account, drawings and photography, and the prescriptions for each level of recording include a list of the numbered items from those sections which should be included. This constitutes a very useful checklist for the church recorder and should be read in conjunction with the more discursive treatment offered here.

Verbal description

A written account of an ecclesiastical building can range from a brief outline of two or three lines to a full-length monograph. For most practical purposes descriptions fall somewhere between these two extremes. The best-known examples are the short but comprehensive entries in the volumes of the Penguin Buildings of England series, established by the late Sir Nikolaus Pevsner, and the lengthier and often very detailed descriptions in the topographical volumes of the *Victoria County Histories* or the *Inventories* of the Royal Commissions on Historical Monuments. The 'Pevsner-style' account may be regarded as a basic model for such purposes as a Sites and Monuments Record entry or as background information to the study of some particular aspect or feature, such as (say) a regional survey of western galleries or nave arcades. For a more definitive account, for example in cases where demolition or substantial alteration is threatened, the aim should be a description of VCH/RCHM standard. Whatever the purpose and the style of the account, however, there should be three prime objectives: factual accuracy, completeness and clarity. It is surprisingly easy for errors to creep in, especially when writing up, away from the building, notes which have been taken on site, perhaps in unfavourable conditions. Authors of international repute have been known to write 'north' for 'south' and although such mistakes may seem minor they are potentially very confusing for the inexpert reader. There is no substitute for taking the finished description to the building concerned and checking it in detail. If this can be done by someone who is not familiar with the site and who has not been associated with the writing of the account, so much the better.

A systematic approach to the building is the best way of insuring that significant information does not get omitted, and many fieldworkers recommend the use of a questionnaire or check list with space to write in appropriate information. A prepared document of this sort not only compels the investigator to record every part of the building and its furnishings. It also gives him/her confidence in retrospect that all aspects have truly been covered: the entry 'none' against the heading 'West tower' makes it clear that the tower has not simply been forgotten, perhaps because of enthusiasm for some more exciting feature. A final description based on such a record will automatically be presented in a logical fashion. A useful way of noting information on site is by dictation into a miniature tape recorder, which can be particularly convenient in situations where making a written record is difficult – in dark interiors, in tight corners, or in blustery weather conditions. It is particularly important when using a tape recorder to work to a well-prepared checklist, because it is more difficult to review what has been recorded than it is with written notes.

The final account may be presented in a systematic way, but yet be unclear to the reader. This may be because of over-condensation, which can make architectural description very opaque, or because of verbosity – especially the over-use of abstract nouns and technical vocabulary, not to mention archaeological jargon – and the construction of long, complex sentences like this one. The reader should not have to struggle with the language as well as with the subject matter and the author's arguments. It is not easy, however, to maintain simplicity of style and clarity as the writing moves from description to interpretation. Some of the concepts and arguments are bound to be complex, and there may be no way of avoiding the difficulties. It helps enormously, though, if observation, fact and description are kept separate from interpretation. If the factual material is treated clearly and simply, the reader will be in a better position to understand the ensuing complexities of any argument deriving from it.

Drawing
(a) The initial freehand sketch (see **Fig 23**, a and b)
Many of the problems of the verbal account, whether basic description or interpretation, can be overcome by the addition of illustrations. These can take various forms. Photographic equipment and processing are relatively inexpensive nowadays, and the place of original photographs in the record is discussed below. Older photographs from archives, such as the National Buildings Record, are also useful, especially for making particular points in the course of interpreting a building. On the whole, however, line drawings are of most value

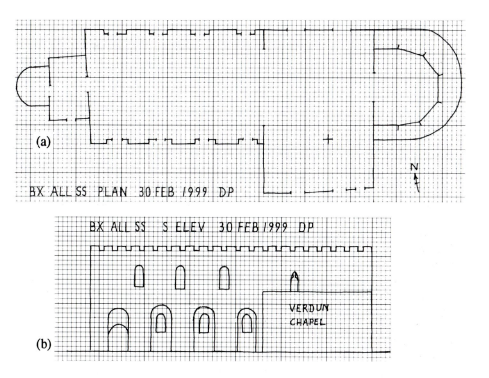

(a)

BX ALL SS PLAN 30 FEB 1999 DP

N

BX ALL SS S ELEV 30 FEB 1999 DP

VERDUN
CHAPEL

(b)

Fig 23 All Saints, Brixworth, Northamptonshire:
(a) sketch plan (b) specimen sketch elevation

at the initial recording and research stages, since they can be so easily and cheaply reproduced, and enlarged or reduced as appropriate for use as working drawings. They may be existing drawings, ranging from old etchings or engravings, such as Fig 22a, to modern architects' or archaeologists' plans and elevations, for example Figure 19. If no such convenient ready-made drawings exist, or if for any reason it is not appropriate to use them, then the investigator has to work up an original drawing or set of drawings, beginning with the outline field sketch.

There is a great deal to be said for producing such drawings oneself in any case. Their usefulness goes far beyond the complementing of the verbal description. They are the quickest, most efficient and most concise way of making a record, and in addition the drawing of even the most sketchy plan or elevation forces the investigator to look at the building with insight. In the course of making a drawing he or she must take in all significant detail and understand how all the parts relate to the whole. In short, the act of drawing is also an act of interpretation, and the committing of a plan or elevation to paper is the first step in making a total analysis of the whole building.

The initial sketch plan need not be very elaborate. It will probably be drawn on the page of a note-book or on a sheet of plain paper on a clipboard. In emergency it may have to be drawn on the back of an envelope or a Christmas card! In the most favourable conditions a block of draughting paper with grid lines at 1- and 10-millimetre intervals will be available, and this will be a great help in achieving the right proportions, so that the sketch will finish up roughly to scale. At this stage walls should be represented by a single line with no attempt to show their thickness. Unless there is some obvious reason to the contrary (eg an octagonal building), assume that the angles at the corners are right angles. The apparent exterior outline of the building can be drawn, beginning from one corner. Pace out the length of the two walls forming the corner. The actual length of the pace does not matter, but it is important to try to keep a consistent length throughout the survey. Lines representing the relative proportions of these two walls can now be drawn on the paper, using a medium-soft pencil. Continue wall by wall all round the building until the lines on the paper join. Doors and other openings at ground level can be represented by a break in the line, and the position of their jambs – again 'measured in' by pacing – shown by short strokes across the wall line. Now the interior can be tackled, and the disposition of the various aisles or rooms indicated by drawing in partition walls and ground-floor openings in the same way. The positions of piers or columns supporting arches can be marked with a conventional symbol, such as a cross, a square, a circle, or a lozenge, as seems most appropriate. At this stage major items of furniture may also be shown in outline.

The sketch plan can be supplemented by outline elevation drawings showing the interior or exterior of any wall where there is any evidence to record. Begin with a horizontal baseline of the same length as the relevant wall line on the sketch plan. Put in any doors or arches already represented on the plan by drawing vertical lines to show the jambs. Estimate the height of the jambs and the total height of the opening by reference to your own height (= approximately 2 paces). Draw in the arch or lintel freehand. Estimate the total height of the building. This may be judged as n times the height of any opening already drawn in, but in brick or ashlar buildings it is possible to estimate by counting the number of courses from ground level to eaves. Draw a horizontal line to show the top of the wall and join to the baseline with verticals representing the corners. Into this frame can be fitted features higher than ground level, such as windows. Vertical features, like buttresses, which may be shown on plan as a single line at right angles to the wall, should be given width on the elevation diagram. Regularly placed buttresses divide the wall up into convenient panels and are a great help in determining the proportions and putting the other features in the right place.

Before leaving the site, it is important to add some verbal description to the drawings, even though a separate questionnaire may have been completed. It is essential to title each drawing with the name of the building, the date, and the name of the investigator. Each sketch should be labelled 'plan' or 'N elevation interior', etc, as appropriate, and plans should include an approxi-

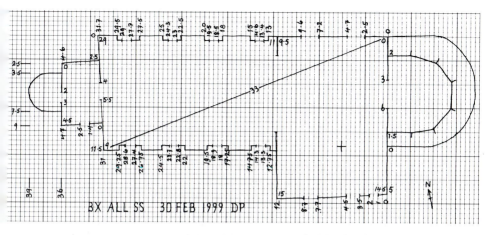

Fig 24   All Saints, Brixworth: sketch plan with dimensions (Note: measuring in the apse and ambulatory is not possible without specialist equipment)

mate indication of where north lies. More detailed notes may be written around the drawings, but take care not to draw arrows or other lines in such a way that they can be mistaken for part of the plan outline. One way of avoiding this is to label features requiring comment with letters of the alphabet, with a separate list of explanatory notes labelled in the same way, as in Figure 25. The published work of the late Harold Taylor contains many examples of finished drawings treated in this way, with the explanatory matter contained in the caption. The labels 'A', 'B', 'C', etc, leave the drawings clear and easy to comprehend. Dr Taylor was a great exponent of the drawing *raisonné*, and his illustrations are good examples of the essential and highly informative interplay of words and pictures.

The annotated sketch is the basic site record and must be protected from loss or damage. Even if it is drawn on squared paper of good quality, it hardly constitutes a permanent record. At the very least the drawing and notes should be inked in with draughting ink at the first opportunity, either in the drawing office or at home. Where the field sketch is on poor quality or inappropriate paper, it should be transferred on to proper drawing paper or draughting film. This consolidated original or fair copy should be carefully kept with the papers referring to the site or in an organised collection of drawings, and it should not be removed. Unlimited working copies can be produced by xerography, and these may be enlarged for convenience when it comes to further survey work on site.

(b) The sketch with dimensions (Fig 24)
The quality of the record can now be improved by adding dimensions to the sketches, beginning with the plan. The essential pieces of equipment are a long linen, plastic or steel tape (30m is a common length) and a hand measure

about 3m long which is, or can be, rigid in use – a short tape, a folding rule, or a telescopic measuring rod. The shorter measure should be used only for recording small features and detail. For most purposes the long tape should be used, fixed – or held by an assistant – at one corner of a wall and held taut and horizontal along the whole length of the wall. There are two major reasons for not using a short tape and measuring along a wall in sections. The first is that it is customary to take measurements to the nearest 5mm or even 10mm (note: the *centimetre* is not a British standard unit of measurement). One reason for this is that it is not possible to produce a higher degree of accuracy than this in the finished drawing: a line drawn with a 0.5 stylus represents 5mm at 1:10 scale, 10mm at 1:20, and so on. Another is that buildings which have been subject to weathering and even unweathered rubble buildings do not offer sharp 'edges' which can be measured with pinpoint accuracy. It is easy then, to understand how the length of a 30m wall could be exaggerated if measured in sections of less than 3m. At least 11 measurements would be required, and if each were rounded up to the nearest 10mm another 44mm could be added to the total length. This inaccuracy could be further increased if each section were not measured from exactly the point to which the previous section had been taken, and where the edges of features are indistinct this is all too easy to do. These factors, taken together, are described as 'cumulative error'. The second reason for not measuring along a wall in sections is that other kinds of error may also be multiplied. It is quite easy to misread a measuring tape, especially in adverse conditions. A misreading in any section of a cumulative measuring operation will affect all subsequent sections and the total dimension of the wall being measured. If all dimensions are read off a single long tape, one misreading is unlikely to affect the other measurements; indeed, the subsequent correct reading of further dimensions may indicate to the investigator that an error has occurred. He/she is less likely to notice the mistake when measuring section by section.

With the zero point of the long tape at one corner, measure in all the features which begin at ground level (eg doors). Features at a higher level, such as windows, can be projected on to the tape by using a string with a plumb-bob attached to drop perpendiculars from the window reveals, etc. The readings should be recorded systematically on a copy of the master diagram described in (a) above. A full set of readings for the interior as well as for the exterior should enable the correct placing of the internal plan in relation to the plan of the outside, but wall thickness can vary, and some adjustment may be necessary when drawing up the final plan from the sketch with dimensions. As a check, wall thickness should be measured wherever possible. This is simply done by measuring through arches, doors and windows. Windows have to be measured in two parts from each wall face to the glass, and the two dimensions added together; the thickness of the glass can be ignored, but figures should be rounded up rather than down.

Not all buildings are square, as will be readily appreciated from the dimensions shown on the north and south walls of the nave in Figure 24 and from the appearance of the final version of the drawing in Figure 25. The shape of the building can be checked by measuring the diagonals internally, though this may not be as easy as it sounds because of the presence of fixed furniture and other fittings. If it is not possible to measure accurately from corner to corner, then triangulations of smaller scale can be made to check angles, using a corner of the building and two arbitrary points at fixed distances along the adjacent walls.

The previous paragraphs in this section relate to the sketch *plan*. The adding of dimensions to the *elevations* is a less simple matter. The sides of features can be taken from the dimensions entered on the plan, but these will relate only to doors, windows, etc, within reach from ground level. Features at a higher level will have to be measured by plumb-line dropped on to the tape at the base of the wall. This is not difficult in the case of opening windows, but places of worship usually have windows with fixed glazing. The only way of dealing with these, and other high features is to use a ladder, and this will require three people: one to climb the ladder and drop the plumb-line, another to steady the ladder, and a third to control the plumb-bob and enter the dimensions on the diagram. While the ladder is in use, the top corners of the wall should also be plumbed; the quoins of buildings are often not vertical, so the two ends of the eaves should be independently related to the base tape. (For this reason it is not wise to measure from the angles of the building at the upper levels). The next problem is locating correctly the tops and bottoms of the features. Floors and ground level cannot be relied on to be horizontal, and they should not be used to measure from unless a means exists to measure their degree of slope. Eaves are more likely to be horizontal, but measuring down from the wall top is difficult. The only reliable solution is to establish an arbitrary datum by stretching a nylon line across the wall and checking that it is horizontal with a long spirit level (not less than 0.5m). Be careful not to let the line snag on projecting stonework, and if the line has to cross a doorway, keep an eye open for people going in and out. Ideally, permission should be sought to keep the door locked while the survey is in progress. Measurements can now be taken from the datum line. Remember to measure down to the base of the wall and up the eaves at intervals to establish whether they are horizontal or at an angle (inside the building check the levels of floor and ceiling). It is useful, especially when the survey team consists of only one or two people, to have a long rigid measure, such as a ranging rod, a folding or telescopic rule, or a Sopwith staff, whose zero end can be held against a high feature while the gradations are read off against the datum line. There is obviously a limit to the height that can be reached in this way, and a Sopwith staff is particularly heavy and awkward to hold inverted for any length of time. A cheap alternative is a light bamboo cane, which can be more easily held against a high feature, and marked where it crosses the datum. The cane can then be lowered, and the distance of the mark from the end measured in a horizontal position using a conventional flexible tape.

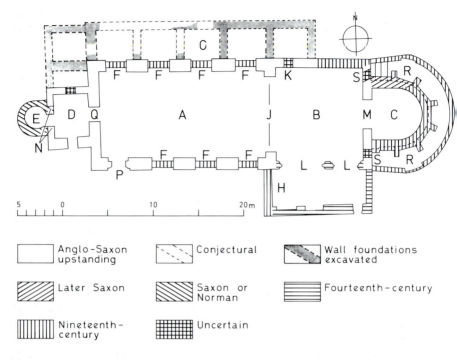

Fig 25   All Saints, Brixworth: period plan. A = nave; B = choir; C = apse;
D = central compartment of narthex, later base of tower; E = stair turret; F = blocking of
arcade arches; G = demolished porticus (observations in the past suggest an equivalent range
of chambers on the S side); H = W wall of chapel as shortened in 19th century,
Anglo-Saxon wall below; J = site of presumed triple arch; K = blocked early door;
L = inserted arches; M = sanctuary arch; N= original great W door; P = inserted
12th-century door; Q = nave W door with blocked opening over; R = ring crypt;
S = blocked doorways originally giving access from choir

Finally, having taken dimensions for the main drawings, some details should be added: shapes of window embrasures, mouldings, staircases, and so on. The positions of these details should be marked on the plan and elevations (identification letters again!), and separate sketches drawn with their own dimensions.

(c) *Architectural drawings* (Figs 25–8)

For most archaeological purposes information is presented as a series of *orthographic* drawings, that is, plans and separate elevations which show only two dimensions (length/width; length/height; width/height). They are effectively more accurate versions of the field sketches, based on the dimensions described in the previous section. Some basic drawing equipment is needed to produce illustrations of an acceptable standard: a simple, but not too small, drawing board; draughting film; a range of pens or styluses with intense black ink; 30° and 45° set squares; a scale rule; compasses capable of drawing in ink, including a beam compass for setting out large drawings; and stencils for producing lettering, symbols such as arrows, circles, and so on. Transfer lettering and symbols are widely used, because they are convenient, despite their high cost. Their disadvantage is that handling, even in storage, tends to dislodge the lettering; sometimes a letter or figure can re-attach itself to another part of the drawing, which could be misleading. In spite of the more restricted choice of styles and the inelegance of some stencils, they are to be preferred to transfer lettering because they are as permanent as the drawing itself. A great deal of useful advice on drawing at this level is given by Dr Lance Smith in his *Investigating Old Buildings* (1985, 108–25).

The draughting film should be mounted on the drawing board with a fairly heavy paper underlay; paper printed with millimetre squares is a helpful guide when laying out and scaling the drawing. The actual scale chosen will depend on several factors, including the size of the original subject, the level of detail to be shown, the size of final drawing which can be stored, and – if the drawing is to be reproduced for publication – the degree of reduction anticipated. A 'base-line' must be selected from which the drawing can be built up. In the case of elevations the choice is easy: it will be the vertical or horizontal datum from which the dimensions have been taken (see p 77). For plans of regular buildings the longest continuous line can be used as the basis for the drawing, but where the dimensions indicate that some angles are not right angles (eg Fig 24) the drawing must be based on one of the major diagonals. The ends of the diagonal line will represent two of the corners of the building or a room within it; the two remaining corners can be plotted from these by using compasses to draw intersecting arcs. Where it has not been possible to measure the diagonals, the drawing will have to be built up from one corner, whose angle must be calculated from the triangulated dimensions described in the previous section (p 77). When the plan or elevation has been constructed from the available dimensions, it should be titled and labelled as before, a north point and scale should be drawn in, and hatching, shading or tinting should be added if the drawing is to demonstrate the structural sequence of the building.

Drawings produced in the way just described are adequate for most general purposes, but there are circumstances which require a greater degree of accuracy. Examples of such circumstances are: the need to relate the results of archaeological excavations to the standing building; the need to plot accurately the positions of parts of the fabric subject to scientific analysis (eg the extraction of mortar samples, petrological determinations); and the desire to present a closely argued interpretation, possibly with phased reconstruction drawings.

However good the draughtsmanship, the accuracy of a drawing cannot be greater than the accuracy of the initial survey. Surveying to a sufficient standard to produce high-accuracy drawings may be beyond the resources of non-

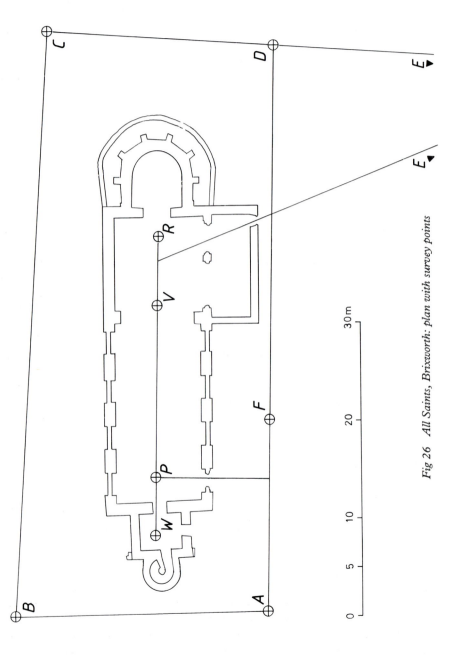

Fig 26 All Saints, Brixworth: plan with survey points

professional groups (it is essentially a group activity), and much of it will necessarily be carried out by archaeological units or bodies such as RCHM or HBMC. Nevertheless, individual readers of this handbook may well be involved in a professional project on a place of worship, either as volunteers or as students gaining surveying experience. A brief description of the principles and procedures will therefore not be out of place here.

In theory, the simplest way of accurate plan surveying is to take right-angle offsets from a calibrated base-line, that is a measuring tape fixed at a convenient distance from a wall. To plan a complete building, at least four base-lines are needed outside the building, and ideally these should be at right angles to each other, forming a rectangular 'box'; baselines within the building should also follow the axes of this box. In practice it is often difficult to achieve such a grid of base-lines. It is frequently impossible to get a clear run for any one base-line because of tombs, gravestones, war memorials or trees in the church-yard and because of fixed pews, cupboards and other fittings inside the place of worship.

The often irregular build-up of burial earth in the graveyard may also make it impossible to lay a really horizontal baseline which is essential for accurate surveying. An alternative method is to set up a number of permanent or semi-permanent survey stations in and around the building, which are themselves surveyed in by theodolite. Key points are then recorded by triangulation from any two of the fixed stations. This calls for well organised record keeping and makes for a great deal of work on the drawing board. Figure 26 shows how a combination of methods was used to survey All Saints' Church, Brixworth, Northamptonshire. An instrument survey was used to locate external stations A to F, which took the form of brass studs concreted into the ground. Their positions were chosen to allow for a clear tape run between any two adjacent stations, and this resulted in an irregular quadrilateral 'box' around the church. An internal baseline was set up in the central alley of the church parallel to the side AFD of the exterior 'box'. Much of the exterior plan was drawn from triangulation data, while the interior was measured by offset from WPVR and secondary baselines parallel to it.

Accurate elevation drawing depends on establishing a grid over the wall surface to be drawn. The use of a horizontal datum line was described in the previous section. For accurate survey work the line should be determined by theodolite. Many places of worship have an Ordnance Survey benchmark set in their masonry. In these cases the site datum should be related to the benchmark; otherwise a convenient level may be chosen arbitrarily. Further horizontal lines should be established up and down the wall at regular (usually one-metre) intervals. The same datum level should be used for all the walls of the building, both inside and out, so that the individual elevation drawings can be accurately related to each other when the survey is complete.

Setting up the vertical elements of the grid may be more difficult. The taking of dimensions for the sketch elevations will have shown that dropping a perpendicular by plumb-line is not all that easy. Projections – from the wall face window sills, mouldings, or just irregular rubble work – will prevent the plumb-line from hanging free, though it is possible to overcome minor irregularities by suspending the line a few millimetres away from the wall face. If the wall has a marked batter, ie, if it is significantly thinner at the top than at the base, it is almost impossible to plumb with any accuracy. Even if a line will hang free, its accuracy can be affected by wind. Tricks like increasing the weight at the end of the line and suspending it in a bucket of water counteract the effects of wind, but the accuracy of a line established in this way will always be in doubt. At this level of surveying it is best to use an instrument to establish a vertical datum. Further verticals should now be established at the same intervals as the horizontals, so that the wall is covered with grid squares. In order to draw to scale whatever features or parts of features occur in each square it is necessary to use a mobile scaffolding tower; it is simply unsafe to try to hold drawing board, pencil and hand rule when standing on a ladder. Using this method it is possible to achieve a high degree of accuracy for the elevation as a whole and moderate accuracy for individual small elements. The stone-by-stone drawing published by Sutherland & Parsons (1984) was produced by the method described above.

Back in the drawing office there is more to do than making fair copies of the accurate plans and elevations achieved in this way. For a complete understanding of even a fairly simple building, three-dimensional representation is desirable. If for no other reason, the investigator should attempt three-dimensional drawing to clear his/her mind about the nature of the building and whether provisional interpretations are likely to hold water. *Perspective* drawing is not to be recommended. It certainly has its place in architectural studies, but it requires developed artistic skills to do it properly. At a mechanical level, it is of no use to anyone wishing to scale off measurements. To make that possible it is necessary to use a simple *projection*. The best-known is *isometric projection,* which gives a similar effect to perspective. The two axes of the plan are drawn at 30° to the horizontal (and thus at 120° to each other); the verticals are drawn vertically. The main drawback is the distortion of the plan, which has to be redrawn from the normal orthographic representation. Irregular plans are particularly difficult to draw for isometric projection. The advantage of this type of drawing is that it gives an equally good view of both elevations shown. So also does the standard *axonometric* projection, where the axes of the plan are at 45° to the horizontal, though the view in each case is slightly inferior to that of an isometric drawing. An axonometric projection is easier to draw, since it is based on the true orthographic plan, which can be used without redrawing. Its disadvantage is that there is a greater degree of distortion, which often verges on ugliness. Textbooks often do not make it clear, however, that the axes of an axonometric drawing can be at any angle to the horizontal so long as they remain at 90° to each other. The convention often adopted by archaeologists and art historians is to draw one at 30° and the other at 60° to the

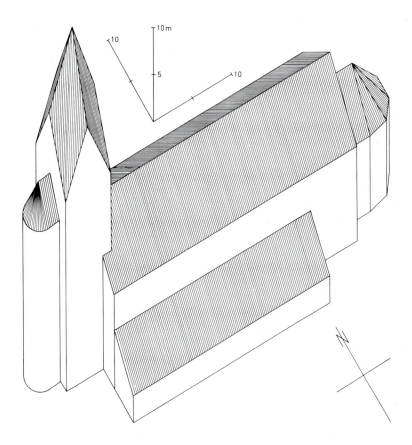

Fig 27   All Saints, Brixworth: 60°/30° axonometric reconstruction c 1100

horizontal. This reduces the apparent distortion but results in one elevation being better represented than the other: the draughtsman has to decide which he wishes to give preference. Figures 27 and 28 are both drawn to this convention. Figure 27 has its east-west axis at 30° to horizontal and gives a view of the south elevation which is equal to that of an isometric projection. Figure 28 is drawn with the north-south axis at 30°, and gives a better view of all west-facing elevations. This diagram is a *cutaway projection,* in which selected walls or parts of walls have been omitted to give a view of the interior. This is a very useful device in interpretation drawing.

(d) Modern survey and drawing methods
The foregoing discussion of drawing methods assumes the use of traditional materials and techniques, and these are largely what will be easily available to

the individual church recorder. At the professional level, however, more sophisticated computer-linked apparatus has become available, both for carrying out the initial survey and for realising it as a series of drawings which can be archived and published. Since the hardware is becoming a more common feature in museums and archaeological units and in university departments of surveying or archaeology, individuals are increasingly likely to have some contact with it, if not to use it themselves, so that some knowledge of the techniques and the equipment is becoming more and more necessary. At the same time, some of the computer software packages are more readily available and cheaper than they were, and it is now a realistic possibility that many individuals will have access to them for use on home computers. In time – and perhaps a relatively short time – the Rapidograph, drawing film and transfer lettering will become things of the

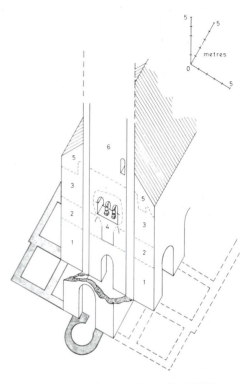

Fig 28   All Saints, Brixworth: 30°/60° axonometric cutaway view/interpretation

past. It seems sensible, therefore, to give a brief introduction here to modern survey and drawing methods. For more detail the reader is referred to Swallow *et al* 1993, especially chapter 9.

On the survey front the EDM (electro-magnetic distance measurement) has largely replaced the optical dumpy level and theodolite. It can be used manually as a combined theodolite and range-finder, and should hold no terrors for anyone familiar with distance-setting on a non-automatic camera and with measuring angles with a traditional theodolite. In fact, the easiest mistake to make with an EDM is to forget to recharge the battery! At a more sophisticated level, the EDM can be coupled to a data-logger to record electronically a large amount of survey data, which can be later processed through a computer to print out accurate (if rather soulless) plans and elevation drawings. The so-called 'total station' EDM is able to combine distance and angle measurements and compare them with the values of targets placed at strategic positions on a building to produce a detailed three-dimensional record.

Whatever means are used to survey a standing building, whether traditional manual techniques or modern electronic technology, the processing of the record back in the drawing office has been revolutionised by the use of CAD (computer-aided design) programs originally developed to assist architects with original design work. Software drawing packages are now widely available and can greatly improve the accuracy, consistency and speed of drawing. More important, they offer new opportunities to produce three-dimensional diagrams like Figs 27 & 28, overlays, matched phase plans like Fig 13, and so on, far less laboriously than by manual methods. The diagrams for this handbook were drawn using traditional materials and techniques at a time when CAD systems were largely confined to architects' offices; they have not been redrawn for this second edition, though it would have been simple to do so using the professional resources of a drawing office on the author's university campus. By the time a third edition becomes necessary it will almost certainly be possible for anybody to draw by computer at home on the kitchen table.

Photography (Figs 29–30)

The camera has long played a central role in archaeological and architectural recording, both in its own right and as a complement to verbal description or to scale drawings. Over the years photographic firms have published guides to architectural photography, but there is now a comprehensive though inexpensive book by an expert, Terry Buchanan's *Photographing historic buildings*. This is both a manual for the practitioner and an excellent collection of pictures of a wide variety of architectural subjects. There is, therefore, no need to enter into great detail here, and what follows is by way of additional comment on one or two aspects referred to in Mr Buchanan's book.

Photographs are generally useful in expanding or explaining what is recorded by other means, especially site notes, questionnaire entries and complete verbal descriptions. Examples of this kind of use can be found in any estate agent's office, where the colour picture has become an obligatory part of the house particulars. Archaeological photography should do more than offer a single generalised view of the building in its setting, however good this picture might be. The aim should be to provide a series of pictures, both inside and out, giving as comprehensive a coverage as is possible. Ideally each shot should include the viewpoint from which another photograph was, or is to be, taken. Photography can also be very useful in recording details which are inaccessible or which there is insufficient time to draw; the subject of any detail photography should also appear in a general view.

It is well known that tilting the camera to include the top of a tower or the ceiling of a room produces a picture in which the vertical lines appear to converge. A similar effect is produced by photographing down a stairwell or when taking the famous view of Rochester Cathedral from the high point at the top of the castle keep. On the whole this effect is acceptable in general photography, but in high-quality record photography it is to be avoided. In recent years 'perspective control' (or 'shift') lenses have become readily

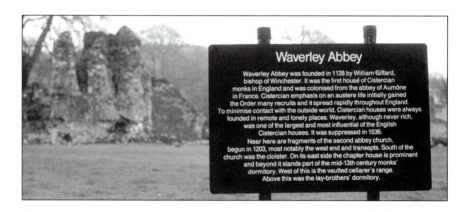

The notice board reads:

Waverley Abbey

Waverley Abbey was founded in 1128 by William Giffard,
bishop of Winchester. It was the first house of Cistercian
monks in England and was colonised from the abbey of Aumône
in France. Cistercian emphasis on an austere life initially gained
the Order many recruits and it spread rapidly throughout England.
To minimise contact with the outside world, Cistercian houses were always
founded in remote and lonely places. Waverley, although never rich,
was one of the largest and most influential of the English
Cistercian houses. It was suppressed in 1536.
Near here are fragments of the second abbey church,
begun in 1203, most notably the west end and transepts. South of the
church was the cloister. On its east side the chapter house is prominent
and beyond it stands part of the mid-13th century monks'
dormitory. West of this is the vaulted cellarer's range.
Above this was the lay-brothers' dormitory.

*Fig 29   The effects of depth of focus: a large aperture (f4) gives little depth of field, so that
the notice board is out of focus when the distant ruins are sharp (top) and vice versa
(centre); with a small aperture (f22) the whole picture is in focus (bottom)*

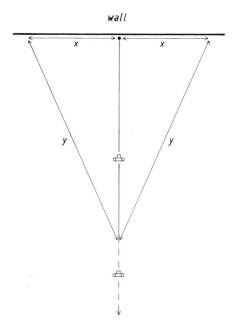

Fig 30 Diagram of camera positions

available for several makes of 35mm camera. They do for the miniature format what the rising front does for the large format technical camera. As well as the movements in relation to the camera body, these lenses have wide-angle characteristics, and are therefore useful where space is limited, even if there is no need to correct converging verticals. Anyone who is likely to do a fair amount of architectural photography would do well to invest in a shift lens, even though the price is daunting, and get used to using it as a matter of course.

Whatever the lens, however, an important consideration in record photography is sharpness, and where there is more than one plane to the subject (which is normal for architectural subjects) the depth of focus must be used to the full. This means selecting the minimum aperture possible, usually f16 or f22 on a 35mm camera. Figure 29 shows the effects of aperture on depth of focus. Since it is also advisable to avoid fast film, because 'graininess' tends to be obtrusive on enlargement, even with modern film, a lot of architectural photography is done at slow shutter speeds. In its turn this obliges the investigator to use a tripod and cable release, especially inside buildings, and to be prepared to use flash or other supplementary lighting.

When photography moves from general information-giving to moderately accurate recording, other considerations apply. The most important of these is to ensure that the plane of the film (ie, the back of the camera) is parallel to the wall surface or the plane of any detail that is being photographed. It is essential to use a tripod. A small spirit level will show whether the camera is upright. To make sure that the sight line is at 90° to the wall surface, the following procedure may be adopted (Fig 30). Mark the centre of the intended picture with a ranging rod placed upright against the wall. Measure a convenient distance along the wall on each side of the ranging rod and mark the points with surveyors' arrows. With two long tapes measure from the arrows towards a point well away from the wall, making sure that the tapes cross at the same distance reading on each. Mark this point with another arrow. The camera may be set up at any position on the line joining this arrow and the ranging rod. If the ranging rod appears in the centre of the viewfinder, the camera back is parallel to the wall. The view should, if possible, include a horizontal scale as well as the ranging rod. The resulting picture may not be aesthetically pleasing, but it will be moderately accurate.

If this procedure is repeated along the length of a wall, with the camera at a standard distance from it, a series of overlapping pictures can be produced, which amounts to a full survey of the wall. This technique, known as 'rectified photography', is described by Ross Dallas in his articles on 'Surveying with a camera' (1980). Detail from the photographs can be added to already surveyed elevations by one of the following methods. If black-and-white film is being used, enlargements should be made to appropriate size. If the ranging rods shown in the photographs are 2m long and the scale of the drawn elevation is 1:20, the dark room technician should be asked to adjust the enlarger to produce an image size for the rods of 100mm. Detail can then be traced off, provided the elevation is drawn on film. Alternatively, if colour transparencies are being made, a slide projector and back projection screen can be used to throw the image on to the back of the drawing, which has been attached to the screen. Adjust the size of the image as with the enlarger, and trace off.

However careful the photography, there is bound to be some distortion with this method, and it should not be relied on as the sole means of survey. The only fully accurate method is photogrammetry, where the photography is done by specialist large-format cameras taking overlapping pictures. These pairs are fed into a computer-linked stereo plotter, which can produce a very accurate result. This is clearly a highly technical process, which is not available to most fieldworkers, and which is also expensive. There are several drawbacks to the method, one of which at least it shares with all survey procedures that rely heavily on the camera: it tends to distance the investigator from the structure and encourages him/her not to look in detail at the fabric. This is a decided disadvantage, because it means that small items of evidence, minor surface irregularities and other details may not be observed, and the investigator has no 'personal contact' with the fabric he/she is supposed to be interpreting. Nevertheless, in ideal circumstances good elevation plots may be made from photogrammetric data, as has been shown in Fig 3, and at very least these can serve as reliable base drawings onto which further information can be added manually.

Further reading
Dymond 1986 gives useful guidelines for writing a generalised account of a place of worship; RCHME 1996 gives concise guidelines about levels of recording and methods of presentation; Hutton 1986 contains practical surveying instructions; Swallow, Watt and Ashton 1993 provide the professional approach to recording historic buildings; and RCHME 1986/91/94 are models of concise verbal descriptions married to illustrations (the plans are drawn with exemplary clarity).

Select Bibliography

There is an enormous number of books, articles and pamphlets on the architecture and furnishings of places of worship, and it is impossible in a publication of this size to give anything like a comprehensive list. The titles noted below have been chosen either because they are referred to in the text of this handbook or because they are useful background reading for one or other of the chapters.

Addleshaw, G W O, & Etchells, F, 1948   *The architectural setting of Anglican worship*

Binney, M, & Burman, P, 1977a   *Churches and chapels: who cares*

Binney, M, & Burman, P (eds), 1977b   *Change and decay: the future of our churches*

Blair, J, & Pyrah, C (eds), 1996   *Church archaeology: research directions for the future* CBA Research Report **104**

Bond, F, 1905   *Gothic architecture in England*

Bond, F, 1908   *Fonts and font covers* (plus many subsequent titles on ecclesiastical architecture and church furnishings)

Buchanan, T, 1983   *Photographing historic buildings*

CBA, 1985   *Hallelujah!: recording chapels and meeting houses*

——, 1987   *Recording worked stone: a practical guide* Practical Handbooks in Archaeology, **1**

Caiger-Smith 1963   *English medieval wallpaintings*

Cocke, T, Findlay, D, Halsey, R, & Williamson, E, 1996   *Recording a church: an illustrated glossary*, CBA Practical Handbooks in Archaeology, 7, 3rd edn

Cox, J C, 1913   *Churchwardens' accounts*, The Antiquary's Books

——, 1914   *The English parish church*

——, 1922   *English church fittings, furniture and accessories*

Cox, J C, & Harvey, A, 1907   *English church furniture*, repr 1973

Dallas, R, 1980   Surveying with a camera, *Architects' J*, **171**, 245–55 & 395–9

Davies, J G, 1968   *The secular use of church buildings*

Department of the Environment *et al*, 1977   *New life for old churches*, Aspects of Conservation, **3**

Dymond, D, 1986   *Writing a church guide*, 2nd edn

Hobson, T F, 1926   *Adderbury 'Rectoria'* Oxfordshire Record Society, **8**

Humphrey, S C, 1981   *Primary sources for the architectural history of Anglican churches in the nineteenth century*, Ecclesiological Society

Hutton, B, 1986   *Recording standing buildings*

MacDowall, R W, 1980   *Recording old houses*

Morris, R, 1989 *Churches in the landscape*

NADFAS, 1989 *Inside churches,* National Assoc of Decorative and Fine Arts Societies

Owen, D M, 1970 *The records of the established church in England excluding parochial records,* Br Records Ass: Archives and the User, 1

Parsons, D (ed), 1984 *A bibliography of Leicestershire churches,* pt 3: *Documentary sources,* fasc 1: *Parochial records, parishes A-H*

Parsons, D, 1994 The church and its architecture before and after the Reformation, in: B. Vyner (ed) *Building on the past: papers celebrating 150 years of the Royal Archaeological Institute,* 264–82

Parsons, D, & Brooke, C J, 1994 Recording churches and cathedrals, in: J Wood (ed), *Buildings archaeology: applications in practice,* 129–54. Oxbow Monograph **43**

Powell, K, & de la Hey, C, 1987 *Churches: a question of conversion*

RCHME, 1996 *Recording historic buildings: a descriptive specification* 3rd edn

RCHME/Stell, C, 1986 *An inventory of nonconformist chapels and meeting houses in central England*

RCHME/Stell, C, 1991 *An inventory of nonconformist chapels and meeting houses in the south-west of England*

RCHME/Stell, C, 1994 *An inventory of nonconformist chapels and meeting houses in the north of England*

Randall, G, 1980 *Church furnishings and decoration in England and Wales*

Rodwell, W, 1989 *English Heritage book of church archaeology* rev edn

Salzman, L F, 1967 *Building in England down to 1540,* rev edn (repr. Sandpiper Books, 1997)

Smith, L, 1985 *Investigating old buildings*

Sutherland, D S, & Parsons, D, 1984 The petrological contribution to the survey of All Saints' church, Brixworth, Northamptonshire: an interim study, *J Br Archaeol Ass,* 137, 45–64

Swallow, P, Watt, D, & Ashton, R, 1993 *Measurement and recording of historic buildings*

Taylor, A Clifton-, 1987 *The pattern of English building,* 4th edn

Taylor, H M, 1972 Structural criticism: a plea for more systematic study of Anglo-Saxon buildings, *Anglo-Saxon England,* 1, 259–72

White, R, & Barker, P, 1998 *Wroxeter: the life and death of a Roman city*

Yates, N, 1991 *Buildings, faith, and worship: the liturgical arrangement of Anglican churches, 1600–1900*

Index

Ilustrations are denoted by page numbers in *italics* or by *illus* where figures are scattered throughout the text.